Sri Mata Amritanandamayi

Life and Experiences of Devotees

by
Swami Amritasvarupananda Puri

Mata Amritanandamayi Center, San Ramon
California, United States

Sri Mata Amritanandamayi - A Biography

Published By:
Mata Amritanandamayi Center
P.O. Box 613, San Ramon, CA 94583-0613 USA
www.amma.org

First printing by MA Center: August 2018

Address in India:
Mata Amritanandamayi Mission Trust
Amritapuri, Kollam Dt.
Kerala 690546, India
www.amritapuri.org
inform@amritapuri.org

Acknowledgements

Many incidents which are narrated in this book were taken from the biography of the Holy Mother written in Malayalam by Prof. M. Ramakrishnan Nair, to whom our heartfelt gratitude is due. Many thanks also to all those who participated in the publication of the present volume.

Contents

Preface

Pradipajvalābhirdivasakaranīrājanavidhih
sudhāsūteshcandropalajalalavairardhyyarachanā
Svakīyairambhōbhih salilanidhisauhityakaranam
tvadīyābhirvāgbhistava janani vāchām stutiriyam

*O Mother! This praise of words in your honour composed
with Your own words is like the worship of lights in
honour of the sun done with its own rays, the oblation in
honour of the moon with the water emanating from the
moonstone, and the pleasing of the ocean with its own
waters.*

– Saundaryalahari, verse 100

Here is a mystic accessible to anyone and everyone, with
whom you can converse and in whose presence you
can feel God. She is humble but firm as the Earth.
She is simple yet beautiful like the full moon. She is Love, she is
Truth, she is the embodiment of Renunciation and self-sacrifice.
She not only teaches but does. She is a giver of everything and a
receiver of nothing. She is soft like a flower but hard like a diamond. She is a Great Master and a Great Mother. Such is Mata
Amritanandamayi.

She was born in full awareness. Having undergone or
displayed (we know not which) rigorous sadhana (spiritual

discipline), she then embraced the entire world with love and compassion of indescribable dimensions, the love and compassion that is her very fibre and being.

From her tender childhood she sought out the Divine Mother and Father even without the guidance of a Guru. She withstood the attacks of her kith and kin, of rationalists and miscreants all of whom tried to destroy her. All alone in the midst of this battlefield, she confronted everything unperturbed and with steadfast courage. At the age of 21 she outwardly manifested her state of God-Realisation and at 22 began to initiate seekers of Truth into spiritual life. By the age of 27, the Holy Mother had established the spiritual headquarters of her international Mission in the house of her birth. Five years later there were nearly 20 branch Ashrams throughout India and abroad. At the age of 33, in response to the invitation of her devotees in America and Europe, the Holy Mother made her first world tour inspiring and uplifting many people around the world.

Above all, she has counselled, wiped the tears and removed the burdens of thousands and thousands of people from all walks of life and from every corner of the earth. It is left to you, dear reader, to decide who and what she is through the intuition of your heart.

Swami Amritaswarupananda

The Legend

In the Alappad Panchayat[1], district of Kollam, Kerala state, South India, there is a small village named Parayakadavu. This village lies amidst an endless expanse of coconut palms stretching along a narrow peninsula separated from the mainland to the east by an intercoastal waterway, while the western shore of the village is buffeted by the sparkling blue-green Arabian Sea.

The people of the village belong to a humble clan of fishermen who proudly trace their ancestry as far back as the sage Parasara. It is sage Parasara who married the fishermaid Satyavati, mother of Sri Veda Vyasa, the renowned codifier of the Vedas. There are many legends told about the sanctity and greatness of this village where daily life and social custom are still closely associated with divine myths, stories which the villagers strongly believe took place thousands of years ago. One such legend is as follows:

Once Lord Subramanya[2], son of Lord Siva and Goddess Parvati, committed a serious error. Infuriated by the transgression of His son, Lord Siva cursed Subramanya, causing him to be born as a fish. Dejected by the fate of her son, Parvati requested the Lord to forgive Subramanya's fault. Instead of consoling Her, Siva became more angry and condemned Parvati as well to be born as a fisherwoman. Later when Lord Siva's anger had subsided, He

---

[1] An alliance of five villages, the governing body overseeing local affairs.
[2] Another name for Sri Muruga, the brother of Sri Ganesh.

9

told Subramanya that He Himself would come and liberate both of them at the appropriate time and thus blessed them.

In accordance with Lord Siva's curse, Lord Subramanya assumed the form of a fish, rather, of a huge whale. Appearing in the sea of Alappad, the whale caused the fishermen terrible harm. Accustomed to fishing both during the day and night, the fishermen could now no longer venture into the seas. Sometimes the whale tore the cast nets of the fishermen to shreds, and at others it overturned their boats, endangering their very lives. The villagers were doomed to poverty and starvation.

The king of the fishermen failed to find a solution. His treasury was becoming bankrupt, as he was feeding the starving people. Finally, in an attempt to solve the problem, he made a proclamation: the person who could catch the troublesome whale would be richly rewarded, and would also be given the hand of the king's beautiful daughter in marriage. Yet the huge whale was so fearsome that nobody came forth to accept the challenge. The king and his subjects were completely disheartened, when an old man mysteriously appeared from the north. Nobody knew who he was. Approaching the king, his back bowed with age, he boldly declared that he could catch the huge whale and save the people from complete devastation. Accompanied by the astonished king and his subjects, the old man walked confidently toward the sea.

Making a long rope by twisting long strands of vines, the old man threw one end into the sea while holding the other end tightly in his hand. The rope of vines encircled the place where the huge whale was lying submerged. Passing the rope to the fishermen, he instructed them to pull with all their strength while chanting a particular mantra. As instructed by the old man, the fishermen started pulling the rope while chanting the mantra. After hours of tremendous effort, the giant fish, entrapped in the vine rope, was dragged to the shore. Suddenly, to everyone's amazement, the whale vanished, and in its place stood Lord Subramanya, released by Lord Siva from the curse. A temple for Lord Subramanya was built on the spot where the giant fish had been shored. That temple stands today as a living monument to remind us of the old story.

The legend does not end there. Now Lord Siva, in the guise of the old man, stepped forward and stood before the king, demanding the reward of the hand of the princess in marriage. The king, who had promised his only daughter to the champion who saved his people, was now trapped in a dilemma. He and his subjects were completely distraught. How could a father, especially as king, give his exquisite young daughter in marriage to an old man? The king begged him to ask for anything in the entire kingdom but his daughter. The old man calmly replied that a king must keep his promise and be truthful to his word

Now the king was in a real quandary. Truth was the strength of the fishermen; they firmly believed that truth was their protector. If one were not truthful, they said, one who went fishing was jumping into the wide open, fierce mouth of death. The king was paralysed; he could neither break his vow nor give his beloved princess in marriage to the old man. At this point, the princess, who was in fact Goddess Parvati Herself, stepped forward and spoke without hesitation: "Father and most noble king, it is everyone's duty to protect and preserve righteousness (dharma). Nothing should stand against it." Despondent, the king had no choice but to allow her to depart with the old man. No one suspected that the humble fishing kingdom had become the stage for a divine drama in which Lord Siva and Goddess Parvati had been reunited. With heavy hearts, the people followed the divine couple for some distance asking, "Where are you going? We would like to come with you." They replied, "We don't have any particular dwelling place (uru); the spot we reach will be our dwelling place (chellunna uru)."

Lord Siva and Goddess Parvati continued on their way, followed by the fisherfolk, finally reaching a spot where they stopped. As Lord Siva stood facing east and Goddess Parvati faced west, the two became transformed into stone images. Chelluruna uru (the place reached) later became Chenganoor of the present day.

In time a temple was constructed and daily worship was begun, when something very strange occurred. Whenever water was brought to the sanctum sanctorum to perform the worship, the priests found a fish in it. This made the performance of the daily worship impossible. In order to find a solution, the temple authorities made an astrological calculation and discovered the whole story of Lord Siva, Goddess Parvati, and the curse of Lord Subramanya. The astrological forecast further revealed that the marriage ceremonies of the old man and the princess had never been conducted. According to the custom, the people of the Alappad coast, where Goddess Parvati had been born as a fishermaid, should come with dowry and other marriage presentations to Chenganoor in order to conduct the marriage. Subsequently the necessary preparations were made in Chenganoor and Alappad. The villagers of Alappad duly assembled the paraphernalia and travelled to Chenganoor to conduct the divine marriage ceremony. To this day, every year during the festival season, this custom is followed in memory of the ancient legend. The temple still remains a centre of attraction to thousands of devotees.

A few decades ago an interesting incident took place in connection with this story. One year the people from the Alappad coast did not participate in the festival by observing the customary rules and preparation, thinking it meaningless and wasteful to spend a lot of money to travel all the way to Chenganoor. They thought, "Why should we cooperate in a festival which is conducted in a distant place?" Mysterious happenings immediately took place in the Chenganoor temple. The decorated elephant which was to carry the Lord's idol in the procession stood still, refusing to take even a step. All efforts to make it move failed. Word was immediately sent to Alappad of this inauspicious occurrence, but too late. Smallpox had already broken out there. Realizing their foolish mistake and with deep remorse, the villagers made their way to Chenganoor without delay, bringing all the preparations for contributing to the festival according to the custom.

Such is the ancient lore which is intimately interwoven with this coastal landscape and its people. Is it a wonder then that this sacred place has again become centre stage for a divine drama?

Chapter One

From Birth Itself

"From birth itself I had an intense liking for the Divine Name. So much so, I would repeat the Lord's Name incessantly with every breath, and a constant flow of divine thoughts was kept up in my mind irrespective of the place where I was or the work I was attending to. This unbroken recollection of God with love and devotion would be of immense help to any aspirant in attaining Divine Realisation."

– Mata Amritanandamayi

Thīrthikurvanti tīrthani sukarmikurvanti
karmāni saccāstri kurvanti śāstrāni
modante pitaro nrityanti devatāḥ
sanatha ceyan bhūrbhavati

*The Great Saints impart sanctity to places of pilgrimage,
render actions righteous and good, and give spiritual
authority to the scriptures.*

*When such a Saint is born, the fathers rejoice, the Gods
dance in joy and this Earth gets a saviour.*

– Narada Bhakti Sutras, verses 69-71

Ancestry

The Idamannel family was an ancient family whose land
in Parayakadavu village formed a small part of Alappad
Panchayat. Though their hereditary work was fishing,
they did other work as well. A vital part of their daily life was
to perform religious practices and to observe various vows. The
fishermen of the family were also known for their generosity. On
returning from the sea with their day's catch, the first thing they
did was to give some fish to all the villagers who had gathered,
without accepting any money. After selling their day's catch, they
would distribute a handful of coins among all the children.

Many pious souls had been born in the Idamannel family.
Sri Velayudhan was such a man. He was a very compassionate,

truthful and generous person, who firmly held the ideal of ahimsa (nonviolence). He would not allow even a little rat to be killed. Velayudhan was married to Srimati Madhavi, a chaste and pious woman, whose habit was to get up early in the morning before dawn in order to make flower garlands for all the deities in the family shrine room. As she worked, she always chanted the Divine Names of God. Even today, now in her eighties, she sits daily before the temple stringing garlands with the same devoted spirit.

Sugunanandan was their eldest son of five children. Inspired by the devotional atmosphere of his family, he became an ardent devotee of Lord Krishna. When he was nine or ten years old, he began studying Kathakali, a classical dance drama of Kerala, which depicts the games and playful diversions of the gods and goddesses. While the actors present the story through dance and mudras (divine gestures), singers narrate the story through their songs. The character Sugunanandan most loved to portray was Sri Krishna. Once during a Kathakali performance he became so identified with his role of Krishna that he fell unconscious on the stage.

The atmosphere around the Idamannel compound was very peaceful and calm. On three sides it was skirted by the backwaters, which were alive with wildlife and surrounded by lush vegetation consisting of coconut, fruit and cashew trees. There were very few houses nearby in those days. Coming home from school when he was a young boy of thirteen or fourteen, Sugunanandan and his cousin engaged in their favourite pastime of climbing cashew trees and eating the delicious cashew fruit. One day the two boys were busily plucking cashews, when they noticed a sannyasin *(wandering monk)* with long hair and beard approaching Idamannel. They had never seen him before, and were intrigued by his radiant appearance. After roaming about the property a while, the sannyasin suddenly burst into blissful laughter and proclaimed loudly: "I can see many ascetics sitting immersed in deep meditation in this place. Previously this was the abode of many great souls whose tombs lie under this spot. Many sannyasins will attain liberation here. This will become a holy place." The sannyasin again burst into rapturous laughter and continued on his way. Puzzled by the mendicant's statement, the boys resumed their play. Many years would pass before Sugunanandan and his cousin would shake their heads in wonder, recalling the prophetic words of the wandering monk.

Before long Sugunanandan became busy with his work of marketing fish. When he was twenty-one, he married Damayanti, a twenty year-old girl from the neighbouring village, Bhandaraturuttu. Damayanti came from a devout family, which performed religious practices daily without fail. Her family even had its own temple. From childhood, Damayanti had led a virtuous life. Her father, Punyan, and mother, Karutta Kunya, were exemplary devotees of God. The whole family atmosphere supported her in leading a religious life.

Damayanti was so pious that she was reverently called by the villagers, 'Pattathi Amma', or the 'brahmana lady'. As devotion to God was her focus in life, she would observe various religious vows almost every day of the week. She frequently undertook fasting and would break her fast by drinking the water of tender coconuts which mysteriously fell from the trees.

Thirteen children were born to Damayanti and Sugunanandan, though four died at birth and another after fifty-three days. The remaining children, four daughters and four sons, are named as follows in chronological order from eldest to youngest: Kasturbai[3], Sunil Kumar[4], Sudhamani, Sugunamma, Sajani, Suresh Kumar, Satheesh Kumar, and Sudhir Kumar. Of these

---

[3] Henceforth referred to as Kasturi, the colloquial form of her given name.
[4] Hence forth referred to as Subhagan.

children, it was Sudhamani who was destined to become known throughout the world as Mata Amritanandamayi, the Mother of Immortal Bliss.

During her fourth pregnancy, Damayanti began having strange visions. Sometimes she had wonderful dreams of Lord Krishna; at others she beheld the divine play of Lord Siva and Devi, the Divine Mother. One night Damayanti dreamt that a mysterious figure came to entrust her with an idol of Sri Krishna which was cast in pure gold. Around the same time, Sugunanandan had a dream of the Divine Mother. As he was a devotee of Lord Krishna, he was unable to understand why Devi should suddenly appear to him. Upon relating his story to Damayanti, he found that she had recently had many strange visions also. They both wondered what the significance was, and whether some great good fortune would soon befall them.

At this time Sugunanandan and Damayanti were living in a small hut right on the seaside, as this was more convenient for their fishing business than staying at their other hut on the Idamannel family property some five minutes walk inland. During her three previous pregnancies, Damayanti had always experienced a swelling of her whole body a few weeks before her delivery date. This was the signal for her to relax her daily routine and return to her own family house in Bhandaraturuttu, where she would be cared for during the delivery. Damayanti was still waiting for the swelling to occur before making ready for the birth of her fourth child.

One night Damayanti had a wonderful dream that she had given birth to Krishna, and that He was lying on her lap drinking her breast milk. The next morning she was working at the seaside, when suddenly she had the feeling that she was going to deliver. Damayanti discounted the sensation, however, since the telltale swelling had not yet appeared. The strange feeling persisted though, and Damayanti put her work aside. For some reason she felt an inexplicable urge to go to Idamannel, and, crossing the backwaters alone, she headed inland. Entering the little hut, she began collecting a few items. A moment later, she felt a familiar sensation and realised that she was about to deliver. By the time she had spread a mat and lain down, the child had been born! Damayanti was shocked. She noticed that the baby was a girl. The atmosphere that enveloped the child's birth was completely silent and peaceful. Other than the initial sensation which had alerted her, Damayanti had not felt any discomfort. Now that she was coming to her senses, she was filled with concern. Was the child alive? She heard no cries of a newborn. Anxiously she examined the child. Now Damayanti was even more amazed. The babe had a beaming smile on her tiny face! The gaze of the child penetrated Damayanti's innermost heart and was never forgotten.

At this moment a woman from a neighboring house appeared in the doorway of the hut. Quickly realizing what had happened, she scurried around making the mother and the baby comfortable. Thus it was that on the morning of the twenty-seventh of September, 1953, a tiny girl child was born in a humble hut of woven palm leaves to the sound of the ocean waves echoing on the nearby shore.

The parents were puzzled by the babe's dark blue complexion and the fact that the child lay in padmasana[5], holding her fingers in chinmudra[6] with the tip of her thumb and forefinger touching to form a circle. They feared that this dark blue shade might be the symptom of some strange disease and that the peculiar posture might be due to abnormal bone structure or dislocation. Various doctors were consulted. The fear of bone abnormality was allayed when the doctors confirmed that there was no such

---

[5] The lotus posture of hatha yoga.
[6] The mudra symbolizes the oneness of the individual self with the Supreme.

handicap. As for the skin colour, it could not be attributed to heredity, since both Damayanti and Sugunanandan were light tan in skin tone. Hence, the parents were advised not to bathe the child for six months in the hope that the mysterious ailment would disappear.

Six months passed, and still the baby girl retained the dark blue hue reminiscent of Lord Krishna and Divine Mother Kali. Eventually, over the course of time, dark-blue changed into dark brown. Yet, when the little girl's desire intensified to behold the vision of Lord Krishna, her skin colour once again assumed its blue hue. Even today, especially during the Divine Moods of Krishna and Devi, one can observe a dark blue skin tone.

Ironically, it was because of her blue-black complexion, that Damayanti and the other family members would look upon the child with great disdain. Their aversion for the dark child eventually led them to treat her as the thankless servant of the family and relatives. In fact, only a few close relatives were even informed of the birth, as not much importance was given to this newborn child. It was a girl, and Damayanti had already given birth to three other children.

Who could imagine that this strangely blue-coloured child, born smiling benignly in a small hut along the shores of the Arabian Sea was, in truth, a spiritual giant come to this world to shower peace and godly love upon suffering humankind? Who could foresee this little one's spiritual destiny of helping thousands and thousands of seekers to cross the Ocean of Transmigration?[7]

From the moment of the tiny girl's birth, the family began noticing unusual signs which would be understood only years later. Typically, before walking, a child progresses through various stages of development. First it lies on its back, then rolls over, then lies on its belly and pushes itself up with the forearms. Eventually,

---

[7] The metaphorical representation of the cycle of birth, death and rebirth.

the child begins crawling and, after some months, it gets up on two legs by holding onto something. All this culminates in the toddling stage around one year of age. This little girl's case was entirely different, as none of these stages occurred. One day, after turning six months old, the little girl suddenly stood up and walked straight across the verandah. Not long after that, she started running, which filled everyone's heart with wonder and joy.

Ambrosial Jewel

The parents gave the name Sudhamani, "Ambrosial Jewel", to their remarkable baby daughter. Unlike most other children her age, Sudhamani started speaking her mother tongue, Malayalam, when she was barely six months old. Her passion to sing the Divine Names manifested as soon as she began to speak fairly well. By the age of two, without instruction from anyone, she began saying prayers and singing short songs in praise of Sri Krishna. Needless to say, the family was stunned, when they happened to overhear her. Over the course of the next year, Sudhamani established the habit of melodiously chanting the Divine Names aloud; to this day her custom has continued without interruption. By age four, she sang with devotional fervour her one or two line compositions, seated before her favorite small picture of the Lord.

From infancy, Sudhamani was full of life and vigour. She was an obedient child, and everyone in the village loved her. Even strangers felt an inexplicable attraction and affection for little Sudhamani. Love for God, concern for others, and other admirable traits manifested themselves in her from early childhood. Because of her virtuous qualities, everyone in the village called her by the pet name, "Kunju", which means "the little one".

Strangely enough, these same qualities later became the excuse for severe abuse and maltreatment meted out to her by her own family and relatives.

By the time Sudhamani turned five, a visible stream of inborn devotion to Lord Sri Krishna flowed from her heart, and before long this love took the form of full-fledged devotional songs. The songs were filled with poignant longing for her beloved Krishna, and her enchanting, soulful singing of these simple, yet deeply mystical songs became well-known throughout the village. While chanting or singing, she would focus her eyes on a little picture of Krishna, which she always kept tucked inside her shirt. Then she would sit unmoving for a long time. This extraordinary behaviour and intense devotion amazed everyone and attracted the attention of all the devout villagers. They would rise early in the morning just to hear Sudhamani's angelic singing greeting the new day.

Ampati tannile

O Lord Who has protected Gokulam as the Dear Child of Ampati, O Lord of the Ocean of Milk, Who art the colour of clouds, O Thou with the lotus eyes, I adore Thee with joined palms...

Please give relief from sin to the sinners, O Thou Who art the colour of dark clouds. Please show compassion to the poor ones in this village...

O Lord of the flute Who wears yellow raiment, Who wears the garland of jasmine, please come play the flute. O Destroyer of Putana, please protect me! O One Who reclines on a huge serpent, O Lord of Gokulam Who has prevented the torrential rain, please make me one with Thy Lotus Feet, thereby ridding me of the pain in my soul.

Even at this age, certain visible traits of divinity were appearing in Sudhamani. While engaged in childhood games or other activities, she would suddenly become indrawn. On these occasions, her parents or other family members would find her sitting motionless in some lonely, isolated place. At other times, they would find her sitting near the backwaters, looking intently into the water or silently gazing at the blue sky as if transported to another world. It was not uncommon to find her sitting in solitude with closed eyes. When she was aroused, her mood seemed abstracted.

Unable to understand the import of their daughter's unusual states of consciousness, the parents would scold Sudhamani for not being playful like the other children. This marked the beginning of a long period of maligning their daughter and misinterpreting her flights to the realm of the Divine. For their part, the parents were worried that her peculiar behaviour might indicate a psychological disorder.

When Sudhamani turned five, she was enrolled as a student of the first grade at Srayicadu School in the nearby village. Even at this age, she exhibited brilliant intelligence and memory. Having heard a lesson once, she never forgot even part of it. She could effortlessly recite any of the lessons which had been taught in the class or which she had read. When Sudhamani was studying in the second grade, she would easily recite the lessons of the advanced grades, simply by overhearing the text when it was read aloud. Her older classmates, including her brother and sister, sometimes received harsh punishment from the teacher for being unable to learn verses of poetry by heart. Meanwhile, little Sudhamani, who was studying in the lower grade, would melodiously sing the poems and dance to the melody like a delicate butterfly. All the teachers admired her and were amazed by Kunju's astonishing memory. She scored full marks in all subjects and was ranked first in the class, despite the fact that she was often absent because of household responsibilities.

Another incident which illustrates Sudhamani's remarkable memory occurred five months after Damayanti had given birth. That day she left the house and the child in the care of Sugunanandan. For some unknown reason the babe became restless and began crying. Unaccustomed to such behaviour, Sugunanandan tried hard but could not console the child. When her crying continued, Sugunanandan eventually became exasperated, lost his patience and flung her on the cot.

Many years later, Sudhamani remarked to her father, "Oh, the way you threw me away that day! You were about to kill me!" At first, Sugunanandan did not understand the import of Sudhamani's words, then, after a few moments, the old incident flashed through his mind and he was once again astounded by his daughter's memory.

Whatever free time she had in school, Sudhamani spent in completing her homework with the thought that, after reaching home, she could use that much time in the remembrance of God. Returning home, the little girl would first help her mother with the household chores. Otherwise, she would forget herself singing devotional songs.

Even from childhood Sudhamani was very careful about the proper use of time. She never wasted even a moment sitting idle. While attending to her steadily mounting household duties, Sudhamani constantly chanted the Divine Name of Lord Krishna. Visualizing her beloved Krishna's beautiful form within her heart while repeating His Divine Name, Kunju spent her days and nights in her own world.

The house where Sudhamani spent her childhood consisted merely of two tiny rooms and a kitchen. To alleviate the inconvenience caused by such tight living quarters, Sugunanandan built a small room alongside the cowshed[8]. This was used as a study room for the children, but it was also where little Sudhamani spent her childhood days meditating and singing devotional songs. There were two other refugees in the cowshed, an abandoned woman named Potichi, who was a barber, and her child. Taking pity on their helpless condition, Sugunanandan had allowed them to stay there. Potichi, the barber woman, loved Sudhamani very much. She would always carry the little one on her hip, and in those days it was Potichi who looked after Sudhamani much more than Damayanti.

Thus we find gentle Sudhamani living in the cowshed, while focusing her heart and soul upon the enchanting form of Lord Krishna. Just as cows were very dear to Sri Krishna, the little girl also adored them. Whatever free moments she had she spent sitting with them in solitude, lost in a divine reverie, revelling in the bliss of longing to behold the resplendent Vision of Krishna.

Because of Sudhamani's loving nature, she was always surrounded by children. Whenever they could, they came to Idamannel to play with her. Together they would go to gather grass for the cows. Though Sudhamani's little friends were not interested in doing strenuous tasks, they would happily join her in order to enjoy her cheerful company. All of them had a mysterious attraction and strong bond of love for her. Having completed the work, Sudhamani would involve the children in various games and draw other children into her play, by her enactment of Krishna Leela, the pranks of Sri Krishna as a child. Without difficulty, she would encourage the whole group to sing in loud chorus the devotional songs which were always flowing through her mind.

Nobody could understand Sudhamani's devotional moods, which were becoming more and more intense. As weeks and

[8] In the general proximity of where the old Bhava Darshan Temple now stands.

months passed, she became increasingly absorbed in her devotional activities, singing with deep longing to see the divine beauty of her Lord. Her ecstatic moods became more and more frequent and were not always confined to the cowshed. Oblivious to the world around her, Sudhamani would sometimes dance in ecstasy while moving in a circle and singing devotional songs. The following is a song composed by Kunju when she was seven:

Protect me, O Supreme Lord who resides
In the city of Guruvayoor...
O Child Krishna, who acted as a cowherd boy,
O Lord of the Universe, Consort of Goddess Lakshmi,
Protect me, O Krishna, the Beloved of Radha,
O Krishna, the Beloved of the Gopis,
O Krishna, the son of Nanda,
O Krishna who is worshipped and adored by everyone...

The family and neighbours were totally ignorant of the exalted moods of little Sudhamani and took them to be mere childish games. Who could imagine that this seven year-old girl, having received no spiritual instruction, was swimming in the Ocean of Pure Love and Bliss? Lost to this world, Kunju would sometimes lock herself in a room to sing and dance ecstatically. Once Damayanti peeped through the door and exclaimed, "See how our daughter dances! We should give her dancing lessons!" Poor parents! They were acquainted only with worldly dance. Never had they heard about someone dancing in God-intoxicated bliss. Had there been somebody present who had studied the lives of Great Souls, perhaps he would have recognized Sudhamani's spiritual states. Even then, who would expect to find such a rapturous state in a child so young? As it was, the family concluded that they were witnessing merely the antics of their slightly eccentric and overly imaginative daughter.

Sudhamani's longing to behold her Supreme Lord and merge in Him continued to deepen.. Ceaselessly she gazed at the little picture of Krishna which she kept safely tucked in her shirt. Pouring out her heart to Him in song and prayer, the little girl would cry out, "O my darling Krishna, I am seeing troubles and suffering all around me! O Krishna! Please do not forget to look after this tiny child. I am always calling You; won't You come play with me?"

The following song was composed by Sudhamani at the age of eight and gives a glimpse of the depth of her spiritual intensity:

Kanivin porule

O Essence of Mercy, O Compassionate One,
O Krishna, give me refuge!

O Krishna, is the story of these burning
Tears that flow unknown to Thee?

Offering flowers at Thy Feet that have
Crushed the serpent Kaliya, I will worship
Thee, O Krishna...
Thou didst come as the charioteer of Arjuna
At Kurukshetra to protect Truth and Righteousness.
O Lord Who preserves Dharma
Show a bit of compassion to us!

O Lord of the Gita, Lover of Divine Music,
Give the capacity to sing Thy song...
O Lover of devotional singing,
Do You not hear Thy sacred Names
Uttered from the innermost heart?

The little one's despondent face and her sorrowful songs captured the sympathetic hearts of the villagers. But the great mystery of Sudhamani's inner life still remained unknown to all. Who could imagine the ecstatic rapture of her childhood devotion? Who could understand it but the Wise?

Chapter Two

The Divine Servant

"Mother is the servant of servants. She has no special place to dwell. She dwells in your heart."

– Mata Amritanandamayi

Kāminīriti hi yāminishu khalu kāmanīyaka
nidhē bhavān
Pūrnasammada rasārnavam
kamapi yōgigamya manubhāvayan
Brahmaśankara mukhānapīha
paśupanganāsu bahumānayan
Bhaktalōka gamanīyarūpa
kamanīya driśna paripāhi mām

*O Treasure-house of Beauty! Thou who thus didst
during nights confer on the lovelorn gopikas that same
immense and intense joy of the Spirit which only yogis
attain, and thereby didst make them worthy of respect
even for Brahma and Shiva. May Thou, O Krishna
of lovely form, accessible only to men endowed with
devotion, be pleased to protect me!*

– Srimad Narayaneeyam, canto 69, verse 11

At the age of nine, Sudhamani reached the fourth grade. By
this time she was performing most of the household duties, as her mother was chronically ill. Getting up before
dawn, she attended to her many duties, and only after finishing her
work she hurried off to school. Returning home in the evening,
she spent in prayer and meditation whatever time was left after
her chores. Always carrying her precious picture everywhere, she
wept embracing and kissing it. Sometimes Damayanti went to
fetch water in a distant place, leaving behind little Sudhamani,
who would follow her unobserved, thinking that she might be

able to help her mother. When Damayanti tried to prevent her from coming, Sudhamani protested loudly. Exasperated by her daughter's stubbornness, sometimes Damayanti even locked her in a room. She would try to frighten the little girl saying, "Here comes a ghost! It is coming to get you!" But nobody could frighten Sudhamani. Though only a small child, she was fearless. This fact also commanded the respect of the local villagers who already had great affection for the extraordinary child. There was a woman in the village well known for frightening small children. When children became too mischievous, the parents would call her to frighten them into obedience. Her name was Appisil Amma, and sometimes she was called to Idamannel to frighten little Sudhamani. The notorious woman would sneak up to the window where Sudhamani was sitting. Covering her head with a sack, she jumped and shrieked, making frightening gestures. Peering through the window Kunju would boldly retort, "Go away, I know who you are. You are that Appisil Amma. Don't try to frighten me!"

Like a forlorn, forsaken child Sudhamani would call on her beloved Krishna. The villagers now considered her to be one who dwelt in another world. Unable to understand the reason for the little one's agony, they used to sympathize with her saying, "What a pity! Poor child! What has happened to her? Tears are always streaming down her cheeks. What a deplorable condition! Was she born only to cry? Is the family abusing her? What has she done to undergo such hardships?" Everyone took pity on Sudhamani and some even tried to console her. Yet who but the Beloved of the gopis could appease her unquenchable thirst for spiritual Union?

By this time Sudhamani's equal vision, noble character, compassion toward all living creatures, and enchanting singing had endeared her to all the villagers. Those who had the good fortune to know her soon found themselves opening their hearts to her.

Fate was not so kind when it came to her own family. Sudhamani's mother and elder brother were particularly antagonistic toward her because of her unusual behaviour.

Eventually, following the birth of five more children, Damayanti's health completely deteriorated and she was no longer capable of tending to any household chores. These tasks, already shared by Sudhamani, now fell entirely on her shoulders. Kasturi, the eldest daughter, was studying in a local college, and Subhagan, the eldest son, was also attending school. Her tribulations increasing, Sudhamani toiled from three o'clock in the morning, as she set to work cleaning the house, sweeping the compound, fetching water, cooking the food, tending the cows, milking them, washing the clothes and scrubbing the cooking vessels.

Such a hard routine was extremely arduous for the child. Even to look after the family livestock and poultry was enough work for one person. Yet Sudhamani patiently and devotedly did all the work without complaint. By this point her education had nearly come to an end. Overburdened with work, the little one could not reach school in time. Sometimes when she managed to discharge her duties and run to class, the class had already begun, and, as a punishment for her tardiness, the teacher made the child stand outside the classroom. Even though forced to remain outside, Sudhamani focused keenly on the lesson, and, in this way, she managed to complete the fourth grade.

However, by the time she reached the fifth grade, Sudhamani could no longer keep up with her studies as well as perform her endless stream of household chores. At ten, Sudhamani was forced to abandon her schooling. From early morning before dawn until late at night she laboured. Yet even while engaged in burdensome work, the little one always sang or chanted the Divine Names of her beloved Krishna. Sometimes in the middle of a task she became so absorbed in her devotional mood that she completely lost touch with her external surroundings.

As noted earlier, Sudhamani's day began well before dawn. If she overslept a bit from exhaustion, Damayanti did not hesitate to pour a pitcher of cold water over her. Soon after waking, her first chore was to beat coconut husks with a pestle to turn them into soft fibre, later to be used to manufacture coir, a local product. Then she began a round of tidying the house and yard, fetching water from the village water tap some distance away, washing the utensils, cooking the meals and getting her younger brothers and sisters ready for school. The next round involved bathing the cows, feeding them fodder, again washing the cooking vessels after serving lunch, washing all the family's clothing and gathering grass for the cows. By now it was four o'clock in the afternoon and time for her brothers and sisters to return from school. Sudhamani prepared a snack and tea for them, then somehow found time to visit neighboring houses to collect vegetable scraps or rice gruel for the cows. Furthermore, Damayanti had instructed the child to discharge any duties in the houses she visited which had not been properly done. Again the child would prepare the evening meal for the family and wash the vessels without assistance from anyone.

Sudhamani was considered to be the family's servant, and all domestic chores were hers alone. In addition, Damayanti scrutinized her every action. When she detected any error, however slight, she hastened to mete out swift punishment. Sudhamani's only friend was Krishna; her sole inspiration was his Name. As she performed her many tasks, the intense thought of her beloved Lord would bring tears to her eyes, and she would cry for hours, contemplating His beautiful form.

Finally Sudhamani's day would come to an end about eleven at night. The innocent girl now had a little time for rest. Still she had no desire to lie on the bed or to sleep, rather she sought only to rest in herself, that is, to be with her Lord. When everyone else was at last asleep, she would sit in the small family shrine room pouring her heart out to Lord Krishna in devotional songs. In the darkness of the night, Sudhamani would cry with longing and sing until she finally fell asleep.

Krishna niyennil karunyamekane

O Krishna, please show compassion to me!
O Lord Vishnu, I adore Thee with joined palms!
Please rid me of the burden of speech, mind and body!
Please protect me with affection!

O Krishna, do Thou, who are the friend of the
miserable, not have even a bit of compassion?
Art Thou dwelling only in the golden temple?
Have Thy shining eyes become dim?

O Ocean of Compassion,
Thou are affectionate towards the devotees!
Thy Feet are the Eternal Support!

Even in those days, Sudhamani's mind was so enraptured that it instantly soared to the heights of divinity, when moved by any heart-capturing sight or song. One day while returning home after making some purchases at the market, she heard the melody of a devotional song coming from a distant place. Attracted by the song and in a semiconscious mood, Sudhamani turned and walked in the direction of the singing. The lament was rising from the house of a Christian family where someone had died that day. The relatives were sitting around the body, singing hymns in a tone full of sorrow. The child's heart was immediately moved, and she became lost to the world, standing motionless in a God-intoxicated mood. Her eyes were closed, and tears rolled down her cheeks. The purchased goods fell from her hands and the people gathered there did not know what to make of the unknown girl's sudden transformation, mistakenly thinking that she, too, was moved by the death of their relative.

A half hour passed before Sudhamani partially regained her normal consciousness. Picking up the fallen packages, she hurriedly continued her way home, but too late. Damayanti was waiting for her angrily, and, in a fit of fury, chastised Sudhamani and beat her severely. The little one was still in an indrawn state and received Damayanti's harsh treatment silently and untouched. What external force can distract a mind which is absorbed in God?

Besides her exceptional brilliance, undaunted cheerfulness, exemplary devotion and poignant singing, Sudhamani was known most of all for her loving compassion for the poor and needy. Although she did her best to serve and please her mother, Damayanti, hot-tempered by nature, never hesitated to punish her harshly for any imagined fault. The particular justification for Damayanti's aversion to little Sudhamani was her dark complexion. Moreover, Damayanti would sometimes catch the little one sneaking off with butter, milk and curd, just like the notorious butter thief, Sri Krishna. What Damayanti didn't discover for some time was that the food was being offered to starving families which Sudhamani had befriended.

Unnoticed by others, the child would surreptitiously slip out with milk and curds, after replacing the pilfered quantity with water. When discovered, she invariably received a painful beating. Often her compassionate tendency was exploited by her brothers and sisters who would also steal food, but for themselves, and then accuse Sudhamani. Though she knew who the real thief was, she never uttered a word, but silently endured the harsh blows rained on her by her mother.

When Sudhamani came to know of any family which was starving, she would pilfer money from her mother's little collection box, so that the necessary purchases could be made. If this were not possible, she would obstinately pester her father until he gave her a bit of money. When these two means failed, then she would take raw foodstuffs from her own family's meagre storeroom and give them to the family in need.

Except for certain childhood pranks and lighter moods, all Sudhamani's mischief was based on a selfless intention. Her actions were the fruit of her natural compassion for anyone who was suffering. However, such charitable acts only inflamed Damayanti, who was quick to inflict harsh doses of corporal punishment. Regardless of her own suffering, Sudhamani found immense satisfaction and bliss in giving peace and help to others. She was not at all deterred from these benevolent practices by continuous punishments. She never let others know what she had to endure in order to render her services to poor villagers.

Most of the time Sugunanandan was absent from Idamannel for days at a time, attending to his fishing business, returning only late at night when all the children were fast asleep. Immediately on his return, Damayanti hastened to enumerate her accusations against her servant child. On one such occasion, Sudhamani, who was pretending to be asleep, suddenly shouted out, "I am not your daughter! I must be your daughter-in-law!" Damayanti was stunned to hear Sudhamani's outburst. The little one's implication was clear; she was reminding Damayanti that a real mother would patiently forgive the faults of her daughter, whereas only a mother-in-law would report so meticulously the mistakes of a daughter-in-law exaggerated ten times over.

Who could imagine that the virtuous little Sudhamani's insatiable appetite for relieving sorrow and suffering would soon bring thousands of people from around the world to the distant shores of the Arabian Sea, just as those dying of thirst seek out an oasis? How can one grasp the fact that Sudhamani, barely ten years old, was creating a wave of compassion in this remote fishing village which was destined to be felt throughout the world?

Though she discharged her duties with utmost sincerity, her mother often warned her saying, "Hey girl, don't be lazy! If you sit idle God won't give you any work, and you will die of starvation. Always pray to God, 'O God, please give me work.' That is how everyone prays." Hearing these words, Sudhamani then adopted the prayer, 'O Krishna, please do give me work, please give me Your work!"

The patience, forbearance and sacrifice which Sudhamani showed were incredible. Her capacity to take persecution in stride, while incessantly remembering her Beloved, foreshadowed the advent of one more Great Soul in India's unbroken legacy of God-Realised Saviours. Although she underwent countless ordeals and was tortured cruelly, she took everything as the benevolence of Divine Providence. All her sorrow was kept in her heart and confided only to the Divine Flute Player, Lord Krishna.

In the dark of the night behind the closed doors of the family shrine room, she would pray to Krishna with tear-filled eyes, "O my Beloved Krishna, nobody but You can understand my heart. This world is full of sorrow and suffering. Selfishness reigns supreme. People seek only their own happiness and pleasure. My darling Kanna[9], I desire nothing else but complete oneness with You. O Lord, didn't You see my suffering today? O Lord, please come! Let me see Your Divine Form! These miseries are nothing

---

[9] A name of Krishna.

for me, but the separation from You is agony." The following song was composed by Sudhamani during this period:

Karunya murte

O Embodiment of Compassion Who art of black Colour,
deign to open Thy eyes.
Art Thou not the Destroyer of Sorrow?
This being so, do remove my sufferings!

In this world Thou art the shelter,
O bright-coloured One with eyes like the petals
Of a red lotus, I worship Thee forever
With the flowers of my tears, O Krishna...

O Gopala, Enchanter of the mind,
I am groping in the darkness.
O Thou Who fillest the fourteen worlds, O Sridhara,
open Thy eyes and rid me of sorrow...

Thus, three years of intense yearning and painful ordeals passed. Sudhamani, now thirteen, still worked arduously. As she grew older, her responsibilities also grew. Without uttering a complaint, she continued her struggle as before. At the same time, her spiritual practices also became increasingly intense. One could see the little one's lips always moving, chanting the Divine Name. Internally and externally the Sacred Name flowed in a constant stream from her heart.

Life With the Relatives

Servants were not available in the coastal area for kitchen work and other domestic chores, as there was much more profitable work such as sewing fishing nets and manufacturing coir. Not only that, the people of the fishing clan considered any work other than fishing disgraceful. Therefore, any girls who had discontinued their studies were forced to work ceaselessly doing domestic chores. Moreover, they were often sent to their relatives' houses to render service. It was the custom for the relatives to ask the parents of such girls for their services.

And so it was with Sudhamani. Her relatives insisted that she be given in service to their households. Finally, giving in to their persistent pressure, Sudhamani's parents were forced to send her to the home of her maternal grandmother. Thus Sudhamani spent the next four years playing the role of domestic servant in various relatives' homes.

Sudhamani's grandmother lived six kilometres to the south of Parayakadavu at Bhandaraturuttu. One could reach her village either by travelling by boat down the backwaters or by walking along the shore of the Arabian Sea. As one might imagine, either route had an intoxicating effect on little Sudhamani. Riding in the ferry boat, she would gaze at the blue sky, softly weeping with joy, thinking of blue-coloured Krishna and chanting 'Aum' in harmony with the humming engine. She would focus her attention on the tiny ripples dancing on the water, while visualizing the form of her Beloved there and imagining His divine play. Entering into a state of devotional fervour, her soft 'Aum' would blossom into devotional singing. Her fellow passengers greatly enjoyed the little one's charming singing, and were not at all surprised by her conduct, as they had always considered her to be one from another world. Losing herself in these practices, Sudhamani never felt the distance or boredom of the trip.

The joy of the boat journey was short-lived. One day when she asked her mother for boat fare, Damayanti was quick to scold, "Who are you to travel in a boat? Are you a college girl? For you walking is good enough." It was during this time that Kasturi had begun her college studies, a rare privilege for a girl from the coast. Damayanti was very proud of this fact and always gave her enough money for all her daily expenses. For a parent's child to become a college student was a great thing among families far too poor to send their children for advanced studies. Even if the parents could afford to send their children, they often quickly abandoned the idea when the children showed a lack of interest or initiative. Damayanti was thus showing a bit of understandable vanity.

Sudhamani, being black and a mere servant, was unnoticed, uncared for and completely misunderstood by her own family. Nevertheless, she peacefully accepted prejudice and poverty, as she was full of the presence of Krishna. She was not at all displeased by the crude words of her mother. Quite the contrary! She was happy to walk along the seashore to her grandmother's house. Singing and dancing joyously in solitude, she thought only of the blessing! The six kilometre walk became an exalting experience for Sudhamani who considered the ocean to be her own mother.

One can easily imagine her walking along the shore loudly singing, accompanied by the surging of the ocean waves. As she forgot the outer world, her steps became slower and slower. The sight of the dark blue ocean and the blue-gray storm clouds overhead ravished her mind. The roaring sound of the ocean resembled 'Aum' and invariably had a divinely intoxicating effect on Sudhamani. Seeing Krishna in the waves, she would sometimes run to embrace them! The ocean breeze was for her the soft caress of Sri Krishna Himself. Sometimes she would cry aloud, "Krishna! Krishna!" Deeply absorbed in a state of supreme devotion, she would move along the shore with faltering steps. Eventually she would lose all external consciousness and fall to the sand.

Partially regaining her normal consciousness, Sudhamani would burst into tears praying, "Kanna, my dear Krishna, come running! Where have You gone leaving me here? Why did You abandon me on this unknown shore? Where am I? O Beloved Krishna, come running before the waves of this Ocean of Transmigration swallow me up! O Krishna, lift up this destitute from the sand of pleasures. Are You not the Saviour of Your devotees? Do You not know my heart's pain? What mistake have I committed for You to allow me to suffer like this? O Lord of all worlds, won't You show a little compassion to this humble servant of Yours? Daily I am waiting to hear the magical sound of Your divine flute playing. O Krishna, please come... please come!!"

After some time, she would return to a manageable state of mind and continue her way along the shore, still singing ecstatically. Again the little one would fall several more times on the sand, oblivious to the world around her.

Karunya varidhe

O Krishna, Ocean of Compassion,
Life's miseries are ever increasing.
There is no peace for the mind...
Alas, confusion is so great ... Forgiving all wrongs,
Wipe the sweat from my brow.
O Kanna, now I have no support other than
Thy worshipful Lotus Feet...

O Krishna, the throat is drying up,
The eyes are failing,
The feet are tired,
I am falling to the ground, O Krishna...

In this way, drinking the nectar of supreme love and devotion, Sudhamani would somehow reach her grandmother's house only to have to confront a backbreaking workload. Yet the young girl would contentedly chant the Names of Lord Krishna and carry on with her labours. As far as she was concerned, every moment of life was an opportunity given by the Supreme Lord to serve and remember Him.

Occasionally, Sudhamani was sent to a grain mill some distance from her grandmother's house in order to husk rice paddy. Cheerfully she made the journey, singing her favorite devotional songs as she walked. On the way to the granary, she had to pass through a section of the village where many families lived in appalling poverty. Sudhamani, whose very nature was compassion, would feel very disheartened seeing their plight. While returning home after husking the paddy she used to give some rice away to those families who had been starving for days. Sometimes her grandmother would detect the missing portion of rice, and thinking that Sudhamani had sold it in exchange for a snack, she scolded and beat her. No matter how much Sudhamani was pressed, she never divulged the name of the family to whom she had given the rice. She thought that if she revealed it, her grandmother would surely go quarrel with them.

While staying at Bhandaraturuttu, Sudhamani was also sometimes sent to guard the newly sown paddy fields from crows and chickens. As the field was in a distant place, this duty offered her a chance to be away from all family members and to spend time in solitude remembering and praying to the Lord. Her every breath sounded with the Name of Krishna. Each step was taken remembering His Divine Form. So intense were her love and devotion, that she often collapsed near the field, weeping.

One great solace for Sudhamani was that her grandmother was a devotee of Lord Krishna, and a portrait of Krishna hung on her wall. Sudhamani used to stand in front of it to sing songs to her Lord. At these times, her uncle, Ratnadasan, who loved the little one very much, used to bring a stool for her to sit on while praying, so that she did not have to stand for such a long time. Then Sudhamani would refuse saying, "Oh, how can I sit when Krishna is standing!" The portrait of the Lord was not a piece of painted paper for her; it was Krishna standing there in flesh and blood. For a true devotee there is no such thing as inert matter; every object manifests the glory of the Lord.

Attracted by the heartfelt songs of Sudhamani, the neighbours often used to come to listen to her. The child's exalted singing always filled their minds with love and devotion. Gradually, they too learned Sudhamani's compositions and would sing them in their own shrine rooms. To prevent the cast of the evil eye[10], Sudhamani's uncle would smear sacred ash imbued with special prayers on the forehead of his niece.

Autumn, winter, spring and summer passed. Sudhamani, now fourteen, was sent to the house of Damayanti's elder sister. As usual, she was forced to bear a heavy load alone. First she would boil unhusked rice paddy, then dry it in the sun. The duties of cooking, cleaning and washing all the clothes were hers as well. All the children of the family were in college and considered housework shameful. They had no faith in God, teased Sudhamani mercilessly for her devotional attitude, and tried to prevent her from singing. What could the loving child do, surrounded by these insensitive people? Hiding her face in her hands, she would burst into tears when they temporarily succeeded in preventing her from singing. Though she was externally silenced, no one could check the incessant flow of her heart toward her Beloved.

As the house lay close to the ocean, all the water from the nearby taps was salty. To fetch drinking water, Sudhamani had to row a small boat across the backwaters to a distant fresh water tap. Sometimes she even acted as boatman and ferried her relatives'

---

[10] A superstitious belief of this area.

children across the backwaters to school. With great pleasure she ferried other people's children as well.

Sitting in the canoe on the return trip, the little one took great delight in the beauty of the natural scenery. Crying freely to her Lord, her longing heart's desire to see Krishna would become tremendously intense. She would question the ripples rising on the surface of the river saying, "O little waves, did any of you see my Krishna Who is the colour of a dark blue storm cloud? Have you ever heard the sweet music of His enchanting flute?" Seeing the waves still rising on the water, Sudhamani imagined they were giving a negative reply. Sobbing, she thought, "Oh, like me these little waves are in deep agony without seeing Krishna." Everywhere she perceived the reflection of her own excruciating pain of separation. Imploringly she cried aloud, "O dark blue clouds of the infinite sky, where did you hide my beloved Krishna? O white cranes swiftly flying across the sky, are you going to Vrindavan?[11] If you happen to meet Krishna, please tell Him of this poor child who is always weeping thinking of Him!" Soon Sudhamani would lose all external consciousness and sit in the boat as motionless as a statue. Slowly regaining her normal state of awareness, she would find herself still sitting in the boat which was drifting with the current. Because these exalted spiritual moods occurred spontaneously, there were times when Sudhamani had to face dangers which could have taken her life.

One day little Sudhamani had finished the job of husking paddy and had begun rowing her tiny canoe back to the house. While rowing, gazing at the sky, she saw storm clouds moving across the horizon. The sight filled her innocent heart with the thought of her beloved blue-coloured Krishna. The next instant

---

[11] The place where Sri Krishna spent His childhood, where even today countless of His devotees stay.

she lost all outward awareness and merged in samadhi [12]. The oar fell from her hands. Her eyes were fixed on the sky and, oblivious to her surroundings, she remained transfixed in complete stillness. Now and then calling out, "Krishna, Krishna!", she was entirely lost to the world. The canoe moved into the current, carried on a haphazard course. Suddenly the roar of a loud engine announced the approach of a large boat which was heading directly toward Sudhamani's tiny canoe! The passengers in the boat shouted in alarm, making a vain effort to arouse the little girl. People standing on the banks of the river shouted, and some threw stones in the water around her. At the last possible moment the child partially regained external consciousness and somehow managed to steer her boat clear of danger.

Another year had passed when Sudhamani was sent next to the house of Damayanti's eldest brother, Anandan, in the town of Karunagappallly, about ten kilometres inland from Parayakadavu. With utmost sincerity and enthusiasm Sudhamani discharged her daily chores to the delight of Anandan and his wife, who even rewarded her with a pair of earrings for wholeheartedly performing her duties.

Compassion for the poor was one of the outstanding features of little Sudhamani's character. Whether she was in her uncle's house, her aunt's, or her own family home, nothing could stop her from extending help to those in need. Many Muslim families lived around her uncle's house, and most were very poor. The little one would carefully pocket various articles from her uncle's and secretly pass them on to the needy families. Though at first nobody noticed, after some time her pilfering was discovered. On several occasions Sudhamani received a beating from her auntie, yet she never felt offended by her aunt's actions. She thought,

---

[12] An advanced state of meditation when one's consciousness is completely unified with the Supreme Consciousness.

"Why should I feel offended? Aversion comes only when I take myself to be different from them. I never consider them to be separate. Even at home my parents beat me. Why should I not receive such treatment here as well?"

Although severely beaten several times, Sudhamani was not discouraged from showing mercy to the afflicted. Her habit of giving things to others continued. Such incidents show the immense patience, compassion and forbearance which were her very nature. Taking every event in her life as a lesson, she offered her life as a unique sacrifice as she prepared her future message of love.

Sudhamani's sharp intellect easily penetrated every situation to extract the essential spiritual principles. She would later describe all the trials which she endured as rare blessings bestowed by the Lord to make her understand the ephemeral nature of the world and its relations. As she explained, "From all these experiences I clearly understood that the world is full of sorrow. We have no true relations, for all our relatives love us only to fulfil their own selfish needs. Human beings love each other out of desire. Nobody loves us selflessly. Only God loves us with selfless love."

Sudhamani clearly understood that to continue a close association with her uncle and aunt would be an obstacle to her goal in life. Finally she created circumstances which would free her from that bondage. One morning she quarrelled heatedly with the family, in order to break the agreement, and left the house. The callous relatives even took back all the gifts which they had given her previously, including the earrings, and sent her home empty-handed. On leaving, Sudhamani exclaimed, "One day you will have to come to me begging. Until then I will never enter this house."

After eleven years had passed, financial troubles arose to plague her uncle's family, and they did come to Idamannel to plead for assistance from Sudhamani. Only then did she return to their house to perform worship and thereby bestow her blessing. That day Sudhamani's aunt bemoaned her past actions saying, "Oh, I never imagined that the little one would become so great! How ruthlessly I scolded and beat her!"

The Supreme Lord never fails to fulfil His promise to His true devotee. In the great epics of India many such incidents exemplify the truth that God is the servant of His devotees.

Chapter Three

Tears for Krishna

*"Having no butter and milk to offer to Thee, I
will offer Thee a little of my pain. O Kanna, at
Thy Feet I will offer the pearl drops of my tears."*

– Mata Amritanandamayi

śrī bhagavan uvāca
mayyāveśya mano ye mām/ nitya yuktā upāsate
śraddha parayopetās te me/ yuktatamā matāḥ
mayyeva mana ādhatsva/ mayi buddhim niveśaya
nivasiśyasi mayyi eva ata/ ūrdhvam na samśayaḥ

The Blessed Lord said:

*Those who, fixing their mind on Me, worship Me, ever
steadfast and endowed with supreme sraddha, they, in
My opinion, are the best versed in Yoga.
Fix thy mind on Me only, place thy intellect in
Me; (then) thou shalt no doubt live in Me hereafter.*

– Bhagavad Gita, chapter 12, verses 2 & 8

Return to Idamannel

Returning to Idamannel from her uncle's house, Sudha-mani, now about sixteen, became fully immersed in her spiritual practices while simultaneously shouldering the mountainous burden of household chores. Even in this land of saints, her tremendous passion for spiritual austerity while facing great opposition, stands unique and unparalleled.

As always her work was continuous worship of the Supreme. Anyone seeing Sudhamani in those days would have gasped with wonder. How could her little body withstand such a heavy load? Damayanti had become even more hot-tempered and cruel, since she now suffered from chronic rheumatism which had been aggravated by doing the housework during Sudhamani's absence. Moreover, Sudhamani's compassionate nature, which had led her to steal things from the relatives' houses, had brought her a bad name. This redoubled Damayanti's animosity toward her daughter. Even when she faultlessly discharged her household duties, Damayanti constantly scolded and beat her.

Despite such harsh treatment from her own mother, Sudhamani held no grudge against her. In fact, years later she would refer to Damayanti reverently as her spiritual Guru. In her own words:

"Damayanti Amma was, in a way, my Guru. She inculcated diligence, devotion and discipline in me. She observed all of my actions meticulously. If there were even a little scrap left in the courtyard after sweeping, she would hit me. When all the vessels were washed, she scrutinized them, and if there were even a tiny trace of dirt, she would scold me. If even a single twig of the broom happened to fall on the ground as I swept, she would not spare me. If a speck of dust or ash fell into the cooking pot, punishment would follow. Mother expected her daughters to say their prayers early in the morning; she would not hesitate to pour a pot of water on our faces, particularly on mine, if we were late to rise because of exhaustion. When I plucked grass for the cows, she would watch me from a distance to see if I indulged in gossip with others. She even hit me with a wooden pestle used for pounding rice. Witnessing my mother's actions, the local people would often implore her, 'Please do not punish her like this! She will have to be given in marriage some day!' But all the while I realized that such experiences were only for my own good."

Readers may feel shocked by Damayanti's heartless treatment of her own daughter, especially since she was known as a pious woman. Actually, this is not hard to understand when we consider that her devotion was not based on knowledge. Many devotees have reverence for the gods and goddesses and regularly perform religious rites, but their concept of God is very limited. God is not perceived as dwelling in all beings, but rather He is contained within the four walls of the temple. Such devotees perform religious rites with an aim to fulfil their desires or to satisfy God. Their view of religion and worship has nothing to do with character building nor eradication of their own negative tendencies. These devotees have no desire to realize God or Self as their Supreme Goal. They worship because their fathers did so, or out of fear of incurring sin. However, devotees with understanding perceive God as all-pervasive and serve Him in all beings. They renounce all worldly desires and surrender their whole being at the Lotus Feet of the Lord. Their ultimate goal in life is to realize and become one with the Supreme Reality. Damayanti had a very limited vision of God and of spirituality, which was reflected in her harsh actions toward her unusual daughter.

Sometimes when Damayanti was about to thrash Sudhamani , the child would catch hold of her hand. Though small, Sudhamani was very strong. Unable to release her hand from Sudhamani's grip, she would then try to kick her. The little one would then catch hold of Damayanti's leg as well. Finding no other way to punish her daughter, the mother resorted to biting her. On occasion Damayanti even struck Sudhamani with a machete used to open coconuts. The mother regularly piled vulgar abuse upon the innocent child without restraint.

Sudhamani could be very bold and impertinent at times when dealing with her mother. When Damayanti commanded, "Don't speak!" she would immediately retort, "I will speak!" When Damayanti said, "Don't do it!" Sudhamani would unhesitatingly insist, "I will do it!" But the more she retaliated, the harsher the punishment became. Damayanti would even curse her daughter saying, "Let this defiant girl be damned! If she grows up like this, she will surely bring a bad reputation to the family. O God, why are You not putting an end to her life?"

For her part, Sudhamani was not at all bothered by her mother's cruel ways. In her eyes all people were equal. Even from childhood, she would call elderly men "father" and all elderly women "mother". This further irritated her parents, who considered her peculiar way of addressing others a disgrace to the family. They would scold her saying, "Is it proper for you to call all these dirty people your father and mother?" Sudhamani would reply, "I have never seen my real Father and Mother. Therefore, all are my father and mother."

The little one was prohibited from applying sacred ash to her forehead. The family members would taunt her saying, "Hey girl, are you going to become a sannyasin?" Sudhamani was not even permitted to dress like ordinary girls. If she applied vermillion [13] to her forehead or wore a chequered blouse or clean jacket, she was mocked. "Why do you wear these coloured clothes and apply vermilion? Who are you making a show for?" Girls should live with utmost modesty."

More amazing than the deplorable abuse of her family, was Sudhamani's unwavering tolerance for whatever befell her. Though at times she was saucy, she never harboured an iota of hatred for her tormentors. Later she would simply say, "Damayanti was not punishing me. She treated me poorly only because of her limited vision. All those trials led me along the correct path, so I have no hatred toward her."

One elder brother, Subhagan, was a veritable terror, not only to Sudhamani, but to the family and villagers as well. He was an arrogant atheist who insisted that women should be absolutely quiet and reserved. His hot temper was well known and Sudhamani became his frequent victim. He would not allow her to

---

[13] A sacred red marking worn by Hindus.

make friends with any girls her own age, as he was convinced that companions would ruin her character. When Sudhamani went to fetch drinking water for the family, she always went alone. If she happened to talk to some other girls, she could count on receiving a severe beating from Subhagan. This rule did not dismay Sudhamani; she much preferred to be alone remembering God without distraction.

In those days there was only one water tap for the whole village, and it ran on wind power. There was always a long queue for getting water from the pipe, and each person had to wait in turn. Sudhamani and the village women would gather there with their clay pots, sometimes standing there for hours waiting for the wind to blow. If there were a long queue, Sudhamani would have to leave her pots in the queue in order to gather grass for the cows. The other ladies, knowing her piety and hard-working nature, would lovingly fill her pot and keep it aside for her.

As mentioned earlier, Sudhamani often visited neighboring houses to collect vegetable scraps and rice gruel for the cows. If there were any delay, she would enter the family shrine room to sing a few devotional songs or meditate. Then she would spend some time with the elderly ladies of the house, lovingly inquiring about their wellbeing and listening intently to their sad tales. Even their own children maltreated and neglected them, just because they were old and infirm. Thus Sudhamani witnessed early in life the transience and selfishness of human relationships. Whenever possible she would take these old women home with her and give them a good hot water bath, a nourishing meal, and dress them in her family members' clothes.

If she came to know of anyone who was going without food, she would give them at least some raw foodstuffs from her own house. Sometimes she would bring home small children whom she would find wandering around, not properly attended or nourished by their own parents. Sudhamani would extend the necessary care before returning them to their homes.

One day Sudhamani was caught in the act of taking some food to give to a poor man. Though severely beaten, she refused to desist from her compassionate activities. She continued in the same way whenever she saw that help was needed. On another occasion Sudhamani saw a family starving for want of food. Finding nothing else, she gave them a gold bangle belonging to her mother which they could sell for enough money to buy the desperately needed food. When her father discovered the theft, he tied her to the trunk of a tree in a fit of fury and mercilessly beat her until her tender body bled. Despite such treatment, Sudhamani remained courageous and forgiving. She was overheard praying for God to pardon the terrible actions committed out of ignorance by her misguided relatives. While sitting in solitude, she prayed,

"O Krishna, what kind of world is this? Even the mother who gives birth treats the child with no kindness. Even she has no pure love for her own family. Where can I find selfless and pure love in this world? Is any love that I see truly genuine? Is it not a mere delusion?" Sometimes sitting in the family shrine room she would burst into tears thinking of all this and would cry aloud, "Krishna, Krishna! I have none in this world but You! My mind is always running after You ,yearning to see Your Divine Form. Will You not take me with You? O Krishna, please come running!"

During this period an elderly man, who was a distant relative of the family, came to live at Idamannel. He no longer had any family or relatives and was in very poor health, unable even to walk. Completely bedridden, he was incontinent, and the bed was constantly soiled. Without being asked, Sudhamani immediately began attending to the old man and took complete responsibility for serving him. The other family members would barely look at him, let alone take on any of his care. Thus, in addition to her domestic chores, Sudhamani sincerely and patiently attended to his needs. She would wash his clothes, give him a hot bath each day, remove his excreta and urine, and administer the prescribed medicines at the proper time. Though Sudhamani manifested an extraordinary abundance of noble virtues, no one in the family took any notice, much less understood or appreciated her all-embracing attitude towards life. It can only be divine paradox that the little one received only heaps of abuse for all that she did.

While she was doing her work, Sudhamani's habit was to remember Krishna by pretending that she herself was Krishna, Radha, the Gopis, or some other personality associated with Krishna's life.

Sometimes as she did the cooking, her heart would be filled with the form of Krishna's mother, Yashoda, who would churn the milk, nursing her babe Krishna. While Sudhamani readied her brothers and sisters for school, she imagined that she was adorning Krishna, Balarama and the Gopas[14] before they went out to graze the cows. Perceiving all this with her inner eye, she wept tears of joy. When she went to the market to purchase household goods, she recalled the Gopis who used to walk along the streets of Vrindavan selling milk and butter. Instead of calling out, "Milk, butter..." they would call out "Krishna, Madhava, Govinda, Achyuta...!", so intense was their devotion!

The Gopis' pure love and devotion for Sri Krishna was always a source of great inspiration for Sudhamani. At times she would imagine herself to be Radha, the beloved of Sri Krishna. The mere thought of Radha was enough to steal her mind and soon her awareness of the outer world ebbed away. She would become totally absorbed in a divine mood and would sing, dance and shed tears in ecstasy.

---

[14] The cowherd boys of Vrindavan.

Kalina kannan

O dark-coloured One,
My eyes are pitifully burning for the sight of
Thy Feet. O lotus-eyed One, come running
With the cows and the music of the flute.

For how many days have I been calling Thee?
Hast Thou not even a little compassion?
What great error have I committed?
Art Thou not the Lover of devotees?
Before I fall down crying, deign to come with Thy flute,
Unable to live as I am without seeing Thee
Who art the sole Reality, come, come...

Fulfiller of desires, Cause of all,
O dark-coloured One, come, come...
Without wasting time and increasing my sorrow.
O Embodiment of Compassion, come, come...

While going to fetch water, Sudhamani would remember the
Gopis who would go to the river Yamuna carrying pots on their
heads. As she washed her family's clothes, she would imagine that
she was washing the silken robes of Krishna and the Gopis. After
hanging the clothes to dry, Sudhamani watched them fluttering in
the wind and thought, "O, see how beautifully Krishna's golden
yellow silk robes are dancing in the breeze! " While collecting
grass for the cows and feeding them, she would think intensely
of Krishna who daily acted as shepherd boy to the cows in the
meadows and forests of Vrindavan. Sudhamani would revel in the
thought of the games of the divine Cowherd Boy and the Gopis.

Sudhamani's favorite time of day was dusk, when she would
wade through the backwaters looking for the domestic animals,
the ducks, goats and cows which had gone astray during the day.

While doing so she would remember Krishna, who used to search for the cows and calves which had wandered away from the herd. If she heard any devotional singing, which is common in India during the twilight hour, she would stand motionless, transported to another realm. This would happen often, and an irritated family member would have to go out searching for the child.

Though Sudhamani was ceaselessly engaged in some work or other, her mind was not at all in the work. Her mind was filled with longing, always chasing after Krishna. His Sacred Names were always on her lips and the very word "Krishna" would bring tears to her eyes. Because she was constantly carrying water, washing the family's clothes or wading through the backwaters, her simple garment would remain drenched day and night. In her own words, "I wanted so badly to see my clothes dry! Even though I had so much work, I would pray to God for more, so that I could always be busy dedicating my actions to Him. Carrying water for cooking and steaming pots of rice gruel on my head caused the hair on top of my head to fall out."

Whatever Sudhamani was doing, her lips kept moving. Nobody understood that she was incessantly repeating the Lord's Name. One day her younger brother, Satheesh, who had picked up the family members' habit of verbally abusing Sudhamani, cuttingly remarked, "Always moving one's lips is a symptom of madness!" Though she overheard Satheesh's comment, Sudhamani was unperturbed. Nevertheless, whenever Satheesh had a severe asthma attack, Sudhamani would carry him on her hip all the way to the hospital, even though there were others in the family who could have done it more easily. Nobody cared about his asthmatic condition but the innocent girl who was always waiting for a chance to serve and help others.

It was very late at night when Sudhamani finished her chores. Not a single light remained burning in her own house or in the neighbourhood. Then Sudhamani would loudly sing to her Lord in the family shrine room. Damayanti and Subhagan would tongue lash her for singing in the darkness and disturbing their sleep. Her elder brother, Subhagan, would remark, "Why do you shout and howl like this? Is it so God can hear it in the heavens? Is your God deaf?" Though she had to suffer punishment and scolding, Sudhamani was not deterred from singing to God in the silent hours of the night. Once Subhagan came angrily into the shrine room and criticized her for singing in the darkness. Quick came the reply, "You behold only the external lamp, but within me burns a lamp which is never extinguished!" Needless to say, the inner significance of her remark was lost on the callous Subhagan.

Sudhamani had a fear that God would punish her mother, father, and brother for beating her while she chanted devotional songs. Therefore, she would often sing softly to prevent them from doing such evil actions. Deeply dejected by the obstacles created by her family, Sudhamani would weep as she sat in the shrine room. They then insisted that it was a sin for her to weep while singing devotional songs, and that this would cause them great danger. It made no difference what Sudhamani did, they would find fault. Poor little Sudhamani! She silently endured everything and dissolved all her miseries in the sweet memory of Sri Krishna.

Even from her childhood Sudhamani never confided her sorrows to any human being. The only one to whom she unburdened herself was Lord Krishna. Sudhamani also had the habit of talking to animals and to Nature, imagining that Krishna was listening attentively to her words. Perceiving everything as Krishna, she conversed with all creatures. If a cow happened to be lying down resting, she would also lie down, leaning against its body contentedly, thinking that she was lying on Krishna's lap.

Looking at the stars, the moon and the flowering trees, Sudhamani would ask, "O my friends, have you seen my Krishna? O gentle breeze, have you ever caressed His enchanting form? O glittering stars and silent moon, are you also in search of Him? If you find Him, please tell Him that this poor Sudhamani is also waiting to see Him."

Ningalil arunumundo

Did anyone of you see my darling Kanna?
You can see Him, but He never appears before my eyes...

The mark of sandal paste on the forehead,
The beauty of the yellow silk robes,
The waving locks of hair with the peacock feather...
Oh, when will I behold all this?
Of what use is this body and this life of mine?
All my good fortune has ended...
For how much longer will these sufferings persist?

'Mother Sea' was also one of Sudhamani's friends, and she considered the ocean to be her own mother. Whenever she had a free moment, the child would slip off to the seaside and pour out her heart's miseries while gazing at the vast expanse of water. The dark blue colour would remind her of her blue Beloved, and before long her external awareness sliped away.

Sudhamani had observed some of the neighbours earning their living by doing tailoring jobs. Prompted by the idea to help others with the money which she might earn from tailoring, she now cherished a desire to learn sewing. In this way, she could avoid the unpleasantness of having to take things from her house in order to help others. Full of hope, Sudhamani expressed her wish to her parents. Damayanti's reply was discouraging, "You are not going to be sent to learn sewing, but will soon be given in marriage to a coconut tree climber!" The coconut tree climbers were a low class of people in Kerala whose sole source of income was gained by plucking coconuts. Sudhamani had often been caught stealing coconuts, which Damayanti thought she ate, but which she had always given to the needy.

Sudhamani persisted, nevertheless, until her parents allowed her to learn sewing for one hour a day, with the condition that she complete all the domestic chores before leaving the house. On those days Sudhamani's routine was astounding. Somehow she would manage to complete the chores which had to be done before noontime, and then race off to her sewing class. On some days other girls from the class, knowing Sudhamani's situation, would come help her finish her chores. In the scorching heat of the midday sun, Sudhamani would walk two or three kilometres to the sewing class. After one hour she would dash home in time to serve the noon meal.

The rest of the day continued as usual with her gruelling schedule. The only moments she had for her most important duty, prayer and meditation, were in the silent hours of the night. Sobbing with longing, the little one would merge in a God-intoxicated state. Returning eventually to a semiconscious mood, she would drift off to sleep.

Sudhamani's patience, endurance and seemingly inexhaustible energy, which continue today, were miraculous. Whatever work was heaped on her she did happily, without murmuring a complaint. Sudhamani felt that her birthright and dharma were to extend help to everyone without being asked. Later she explained, "My joy lay in seeing others' happiness. I never thought of my own comfort and workload. Whenever I had the opportunity to serve others, I tried my best to assist them with utmost sincerity and love."

Initially Sudhamani studied sewing in two separate places. After some time she chose to attend the classes which were given in a parochial workshop in a nearby chapel. Quickly learning the mechanics of sewing, she began doing small tailoring jobs for the poor ladies in the neighbourhood. At first she refused to accept money for her services, as this was not her way of doing things. Yet when her parents refused to pay the course fee for her classes, she was compelled to accept wages for her labour. Thus she managed to pay the class fee and used what remained to help the destitute villagers. She was also able to buy a few essential items for doing her sewing tasks. Sudhamani was adept at tailoring and earned a good wage. Without giving even a paise[15] to her house, she used her earnings only to help the poor.

While sewing in the chapel workshop, Sudhamani became immersed in devotional singing and shed tears which would fall on the sewing machine. The priest of the church was a pious, elderly man who took quick notice of Sudhamani's remarkable character. While the other girls gossiped, Sudhamani was absorbed in her devotion. The priest was deeply touched by this, and Sudhamani became very dear to him. This created jealousy among the other girls, yet the little one would show affection to them just as before, without a trace of animosity.

Satheesh always accompanied his sister to class, waiting for her in the church grounds or sitting in a corner. One day during prayer time Sudhamani asked, "Why are you not participating in the prayer?" He replied, "Are we not Hindus?" Sudhamani told him, "You ask the priest if you can also participate in the prayer." The priest happily agreed. From then on Satheesh always attended the prayers.

When her sewing was completed, Sudhamani would go to the church graveyard to do her embroidery. She loved the solitude

---

[15] Equivalent of a penny.

there. Sitting in the graveyard she questioned the departed souls: "How is your life? Where are you living? Are you happy there? Do you have any feelings?" She clearly felt their company and sought to console them. A friend of Sudhamani's elder sister, Kasturi, was buried in that cemetery. The girl had shown boundless love for Sudhamani even when her family was terribly abusing her. Perhaps this was another reason that Sudhamani liked visiting the graveyard. She would talk to the souls drifting along in their subtle bodies and would sing a sorrowful melody for their peaceful rest. Sometimes while sitting in meditation, Sudhamani entered into samadhi in the silence and stillness of the Christian graveyard.

If there were any time remaining after completing her embroidery work, Sudhamani would return to the chapel, which had an inner apartment like a cave. In the dim light, she would gaze upon the crucified form of Jesus Christ. Seeing Jesus on the cross, she felt Him to be her beloved Krishna. Immediately, she would become enraptured. Returning to the plane of normal consciousness, she would weep, thinking of the love and sacrifice of Jesus Christ and Krishna. She would think, "'O, how They have sacrificed everything for the world! People turned against Them, but still They loved them. If They have done it, then why can't I? There is nothing new in it."

Sudhamani was acutely aware of the extreme poverty of the villagers. Seeing their sorrows and sufferings, the little one would weep in the silent hours she spent in the shrine room. She would pray, "O God, is this life? People are toiling day in and day out just for a bit of food to satisfy their hunger. O Krishna, why do you allow them to starve? Why do they become afflicted with diseases? Everywhere I turn I come face to face with selfishness and people's sufferings caused by it. Youngsters pray for a long life and children pray for an early death for their aged father and mother. Nobody is at all interested to care for the elderly. O Lord, what kind of a world is this? What is the purpose of creating such a world? O Krishna, what is the solution for all this?" Such were the prayers of the innocent girl.

Three years had passed when Sudhamani decided to discontinue her tailoring classes, considering them to be a distraction from her spiritual practices which she wanted to intensify. At that time the priest was also transferred to another parish. Before he left, he sent a few of the girls from the class to Idamannel to express his wish to bid farewell to Sudhamani. Accompanied by Satheesh, she went to visit the priest for the last time. Gazing at the child, the priest burst into tears and wept. Sudhamani stood with subdued emotions. The priest said, "Daughter, I am going to give up this job now. I have decided to lead the life of a sannyasin." As Sudhamani and Satheesh were about to leave, the priest said to Satheesh, "You will see, Sudhamani will become great in the future." Perhaps the perceptive priest had already become aware of the shining divinity within the little one.

Having now mastered stitching, Sudhamani expressed her wish to have a machine of her own. Damayanti scolded her for being ambitious, but Sugunanandan promised several times that he would get a machine for her. However, the sewing machine never materialized. Sudhamani decided, "I won't ask for a machine again. Only if God gives one I will use it." After several years, when devotees began flocking to Idamannel, one of her Dutch devotees named Peter purchased a sewing machine for her, and she was reminded of her vow. God cares for every need of His true devotee.

All the children except Sudhamani were studying either in secondary school or college. They all were light in complexion and fair looking. Sudhamani's dark blue complexion and hard working nature made them all look down on her as a mere servant. She was not even given enough clothing. Seeing all these hardships of young Sudhamani and the antagonism of her parents and elder brother, the villagers would say, "Sudhamani was purchased in Kollam[16] in exchange for some paddy husk." Her parents would take all the children to the temples for festivals and other ceremonies, but always ignored Sudhamani and left her behind.

One day, Sudhamani received a chequered blouse and happily put it on. Her elder brother ordered her to remove it instantly. Snatching it from her hand, he set it on fire right in front of her shouting, "Only to attract the attention of others you wear these coloured clothes!" Another time, Damayanti abused her for wearing a yellow silk jacket which belonged to one of her sisters. From then on, she decided that she would wear only clothes provided by the Lord, only old, worn out ones discarded by others. Sudhamani would cut these clothes up to make a blouse and skirt from them. She used the loose threads from an old clothesline to stitch the scraps of cloth together and felt happy not to be a burden to anyone. About those days she later said, "Without having proper thread, scissors or a sewing machine I would somehow manage to stitch my own clothes!"

---

[16] A coastal city 35 kilometres south of Parayakadavu.

Chapter Four

The Real Flute

"The Real Flute is within. Try to enjoy playing it. Once that sound is heard, one can be without death and birth."

– Mata Amritanandamayi

Vaggadgadā dravatē yasya cittam
rudatyabhīshnam hasati kvacicca
vilajja udgāyati nrityatē ca
madbhaktiyuktō bhuvanam punāti

*The devotee whose voice is choked with emotion, whose
heart melts out of Love, who sobs again and again, and
at times begins to laugh, and shaking off bashfulness
begins to sing loudly and dance, sanctifies the whole
world.*

– Srimad Bhagavatam, skanda X, canto XIV, verse 24

Spiritual glory and the strange behaviour of a God-Realised
Soul are far beyond the understanding of the consciousness
of an ordinary human being. Some people consider the
thirst for God as madness, others call it psychological repression,
and still others refuse to accept its reality altogether. The Great
Souls remain unperturbed. They never heed the senseless remarks
of skeptics and critics who cannot be blamed for their limited
perception of the subtle realms of consciousness. Is the physicist
concerned because the man on the street scorns the existence of
subatomic particles? Is he vexed by their baseless criticism?

No scoffing, no mockery, no derision had any effect on the
saintly Sudhamani. As she reached her late teens, she was immersed in an unbroken stream of spiritual awareness. Her devotion to Sri Krishna was indescribably intense. Sudhamani would
naturally and spontaneously ascend from one plane of consciousness to the next. As if to compensate for the heavy work load, her

heart's longing incessantly poured forth in the form of poignant devotional songs which she would go on singing day and night.

Niramilla

A rainbow without colours, a flower without fragrance, when such is my heart, why cry for compassion?

Life has become full of coldness, without even a trace of warmth, like a veena which has no sweet melody, but sorrowful silence alone...

Can the lotus flowers in a small rivulet deep within the forest blossom where the rays of the Sun cannot reach?

Seeing the clouds in the sky, the peacock spreads its wings to dance, but in vain, and a chataka bird[17] waits for drops of water...

Unable to grasp the significance of her rapturous devotional moods, Sudhamani's parents and elder brother would chastise and torture her mercilessly. They were convinced that all her godly activities were symptoms of some mental weakness or depression.

Sudhamani now spent her days and nights meditating, singing, and repeating the Divine Name. Often she would lock herself in the family shrine room and dance in ecstasy to the great disgust of her elder brother. At other times she would cry, overwhelmed by the pain of separation, and later be found unconscious in the sand. One can only wonder how her love for Krishna could continue to increase, for this love of hers knew no bounds. Her

---

[17] It is said that the chataka bird will drink only raindrops that fall during the rains. It does not relish any other water. The idea is that both the peacock and the chataka feel happy at the sight of clouds but become miserable in the absence of rain. Likewise, waiting for God alone to make one happy seems to be in vain after prolonged fruitless search and spiritual practice.

heart's gate stood wide open, and Sudhamani eagerly awaited the appearance of her Lord. How can one possibly describe the intensity of her dedication and self-surrender?

Sudhamani had an unquenchable thirst to hear the tales of Sri Krishna; whenever she overheard someone narrating His stories, her attention was immediately absorbed in Him, and she would enter into samadhi. Long after the story had ended, Sudhamani would sit motionless. By now the villagers found nothing strange or surprising in her otherworldly behaviour. Sometimes Sudhamani would call small children aside and encourage them to enact the stories of Krishna. She would watch their plays with tears in her eyes, and during their storytelling would imagine that Krishna was sitting by her side narrating the tales. Forgetting the circumstances, she would hug the small children, thinking they were really Krishna Himself. Unaccustomed to such behaviour and unfamiliar with Sudhamani's unusual moods, the youngsters would occasionally become frightened. It became the innocent girl's habit to worship small children by offering them naivedyam[18] and delicacies while singing prayers, genuinely seeing them as Sri Krishna.

If anyone happened to be awake in the silent hours of the night, he could hear the pitiful entreaties of the little one appealing to her Lord,

"Krishna, Krishna! My life's goal! When will I behold Your beautiful Form? Will my life and all my effort to see You end in vain? Are my prayers to become united with You unheard? O Krishna, You are said to be full of compassion for Your devotees. Have I displeased your merciful heart? Am I undeserving of being Your servant? For how many days will these prayers go unanswered? Do you feel no compassion for this lowly, forsaken

---

[18] A meal offered to God or the deity in a temple before being given to the devotees to eats.

child? O Kanna, have You also abandoned me? Where are You?... Where are You?..."

Finally she would collapse on the ground, but her nights remained sleepless. She waited and waited without closing her eyes, expecting that the Lord would come at any moment.

Sometimes Sudhamani would sculpt an image of Krishna out of clay and offer worship to it. She would mentally confide to her Beloved, "See, nobody has taught me how to serve You and how to worship You. Please forgive my errors!" Then, for lack of flowers, she would offer sand at the feet of the image. When the worship was over she would feel that Krishna Himself had arrived and was standing right in front of her. With trembling body and tear-filled eyes, Sudhamani would become overwhelmed with devotion and prostrate again and again before the clay image. The next moment she would feel that Krishna was about to run away, and in haste she would jump forward to catch hold of Him. Then she would realize that the whole play was only her imagination and that the clay idol was still only clay. Dissolving in tears and sobbing in dismay, she continued imploring Him, "Krishna, Krishna! Please come and bless this one who is being torn to pieces with longing for Your vision! Is this all to test my love for You? Why do You hesitate? O Kanna, I can endure any torment except this separation from You. O Krishna, has Your heart lost all its compassion?"

Sudhamani was not to be discouraged. Full of eager anticipation, the humble girl confidently waited for the arrival of her Lord. Sometimes she considered herself to be the beloved of Krishna, while at other times she was His servant. This unlettered child, who hadn't studied past the fourth grade and had never read the Vedas or Upanishads, became the embodiment of supreme devotion to Lord Krishna. Different aspects of supreme devotion spontaneously manifested in young Sudhamani.

At this point, the financial affairs of the family took a sharp turn for the worse, as Sugunanandan suffered a great loss in his fish marketing business. Damayanti and the family became very desperate. One day Damayanti told Sudhamani, "Why is God giving us sorrow? Daughter, pray for your father. All his businesses have ended in failure. Sudhamani thought, "O Krishna, how does sorrow begin? What is the root cause of it? Mother is dejected because she desires happiness from her husband and wishes to live comfortably. Is it not desire which brings unhappiness? O darling Krishna, let me not get entangled in it! If I depend on human beings who are immersed in desire and ignorance, then surely I too will become sorrowful. O Krishna, let my mind always cling to Your Lotus Feet!"

During this time, despite their financial trouble, Sudhamani's parents decided to get her married somehow. Damayanti had always been very particular about the raising of her four daughters and her conceit on this point was no secret among the villagers. Her daughters should be perceived as upstanding and virtuous by the community. If their reputations were damaged, then everything was lost in Damayanti's eyes. Toward this end, Damayanti brought up her daughters with extremely strict discipline. They were not permitted to talk to any men, especially young men.

In those days all four sides of Idamannel were surrounded by water, yet Damayanti had a fence built around the house for further protection from intruders. Even then she was not satisfied, so she kept a dog in the house in order to give warning if anyone came near. When the dog barked, she would call Subhagan to see who it was. If it were a stranger or a young man, the brother refused to open the door. Damayanti was always worried about her grownup daughters. Hence she was eager to be rid of Sudhamani, a big part of her burden.

Sugunanandan and Subhagan finally found a suitable bridegroom for Sudhamani, and a day was arranged for the first meeting to take place. In this way the parents could make sure that the young people liked each other before the marriage was performed. The arrangements were made without Sudhamani's knowledge or consent. Not only that, the meeting was to take place in another house, far away from Idamannel. On the chosen day, a lady came to Sudhamani's home on the pretext of employing her to do a tailoring job. She asked Sudhamani to accompany her to her house in order to take all the measurements for her daughters' skirts and blouses.

When Sudhamani arrived at the house, she understood that their intention was entirely different. Offering her a glass of tea, the lady said, "Look here, Sudhamani, there is someone sitting in the next room. Give this tea to him." This is the customary way of introducing a bride to her groom. Clearly knowing their secret intent, Sudhamani replied in a serious tone, "I cannot. I have come to take measurements, not to serve tea." Walking out of the house, she returned home and told Damayanti about the incident. Only then did she understand that all the arrangements had, in fact, been made by her own parents and elder brother.

Another marriage proposal came for Sudhamani. This time the bridegroom and his party were to come to Idamannel. When the prospective husband arrived, Damayanti sweetly asked Sudhamani to bring some bananas for him. In the guests' presence the unwilling bride retorted, "I won't do it! If you want, you can go buy bananas for him!" That was the end of that proposal!

But the parents refused to give up their idea. Still another proposal came for Sudhamani, and it was arranged again for the groom to visit Idamannel. Beforehand, Damayanti approached Sudhamani pleading and crying, "Daughter, please don't bring a bad reputation upon us. Please act politely to your future husband." When the expectant youth arrived to meet Sudhamani, he sat quietly in the living room. Sudhamani was busy in the kitchen pounding dried red chillies with a wooden pestle. She had already decided to face the situation in a more crude way than before. Holding the pestle with both hands like a soldier ready to attack his enemy with a bayonet, Sudhamani stood screaming, threatening him by waving the pestle, and making ridiculous gestures. Damayanti nearly fainted from shame, but the little one was not ready to give up so easily. She continued her drama until the bridegroom's party fled the house, thinking that she was insane. Sudhamani, of course, promptly received her punishment of harsh kicks and blows.

After this incident, Sudhamani decided that if her parents again disturbed her with marriage proposals, she would quit the house and continue her devotional practices in a cave or some other lonely place. In this matter of marriage she was determined, but she had faith that her parents would not make another attempt for a long time.

The family's ill treatment continued to worsen. Unwilling to endure the situation any longer, Sudhamani decided to run away from home. On the same day, a scrap of newspaper, blown by the wind, fell on the ground right in front of her. She picked it up and, to her astonishment, found that it was a clipping which reported the terrible fate of a girl who had run away from home. Taking this as an obvious communication from God, Sudhamani gave up the idea of leaving the house.

On another occasion, the fierce harassment by her family members led her to decide to put an end to her life by jumping into the sea. Considering this idea, she thought, "Who is dying? Who is taking birth? Who can harass a true devotee of the Lord?" This strong conviction chased the thought of dying from her mind.

During those days of intense sadhana, Sudhamani could not sleep in any other house or eat food prepared in a worldly person's kitchen. If she happened to eat such food, she became extremely restless or vomited. For this reason, most days Sudhamani would fast. If she tried to stay in some other house, where worldly people had slept, she could not get a moment of rest. Yet, she was not bothered about sleep, as she preferred to stay awake to meditate and call on her Beloved. She even had a fear of falling asleep, lest Krishna come at that moment and she miss the long-awaited Vision of His Divine Form.

Even at this stage, Sudhamani somehow managed to discharge her household duties without fail. Because of her continuous toilsome work, the villagers nicknamed her "Kaveri". Kaveri was an ideal character endowed with all virtues. Even if she were ill, she would go from house to house selling milk. Seeing her terrible hardships and her noble qualities, the villagers had immense respect and love for Sudhamani.

The bitter experiences of life which she had to face and the brutal environment in which she grew up convinced Sudhamani of the fleeting and selfish nature of worldly life. Only deep contemplation of life and its goal occupied her mind. Contemplating the mystery of life, she would think, 'O God, do You not see all these sorrows and sufferings? Am I alone in this world? Who is my real relative? Who is my Father and who is my Mother? Where is the Truth in all of this? If one takes a human body, is one destined to suffer?" Sudhamani always had sympathy for ordinary people who craved the momentary pleasures of worldly life. She would pray for them, "O Lord, please save those who suffer from ignorance, mistaking the ephemeral world for something great. Please give them right knowledge."

Cows were very dear to Damayanti. Even if the family members had to suffer, she would not allow the cows to undergo any hardship. In her eyes, cows were equal to God. During the season of the southwest monsoons, the Kerala backwaters would overflow the river banks and become one with the Arabian Sea, causing flooding all along the coast. At Idamannel, the family cowshed would succumb to the rising floodwater, and during those times Damayanti would herd the cows inside the house! The living room would become filled with cow dung and urine. All the family members would protest, cursing Damayanti, except Sudhamani of course, who loved the cows even more than her mother did because of the affectionate role they played in the life of Sri Krishna.

To her all seasons were equally inspiring; for her everything was the Divine Play. She was not at all worried about the scorching heat of summer, the heavy downpour of the monsoon season, nor the chilling ocean breezes of winter. She could see nothing in Nature but her Beloved. She had nothing to gain from this world; her sole aim was to merge in the Lotus Feet of Sri Krishna. Even the sound of the rain falling would fill Sudhamani's heart with love. For her, all sounds resembled the sacred syllable, 'Aum', especially that of the falling rain. She would sing the praises of her Lord in consonance with that sound. Happily she would watch the rain, visualizing Krishna standing in each raindrop.

As Sudhamani's spiritual practices intensified, her abstracted moods became more and more noticeable. Sometimes she would enter the bathroom for a shower, but would be discovered there hours later, oblivious to the surroundings. These states of Sudhamani were a mystery to the family who were convinced that she was suffering from some kind of mental aberration. The little one was a lonely traveller in her own world. How can we imagine the spiritual depth of this innocent girl whose love knew no bounds? What force but God Himself was leading her deeper and deeper toward Self-Realisation?

Often, while collecting leaves to feed the goats, Sudhamani was accompanied by small companions who always followed her wherever she went. They loved her company; Sudhamani was their leader. Sitting on a branch of a tree plucking leaves, Sudhamani would become overpowered with the distinct feeling that she herself was Krishna. She later recalled, "All the boys and girls standing below me seemed to be the Gopas and Gopis."

She had many divine visions. Krishna would come late at night and appear before her. The Divine Flute Player would catch hold of her hands and dance with her. At other times, He would play with her and make her laugh. In those blissful moments, she would dance like never before in divine ecstasy, the dance of Radha and Krishna. At these times, she would hear the enchanting sound of Krishna's flute. At first, she thought that Krishna was playing His heavenly flute standing somewhere nearby, but then realised with astonishment that the sound was coming from within her! Immediately she would burst into tears and collapse in front of Sri Krishna's portrait. If she happened to sleep, within no time Krishna would appear to wake her. Sudhamani later remarked, "His complexion was a combination of dark blue and light red." Sometimes she saw a cot spread with different kinds of fragrant flowers. Catching hold of the little one's hands, Krishna would dance on it with her. He would take her up above the clouds and show her different worlds and beautiful scenery. But Sudhamani thought, "What attraction do these things have if He is not there? He is the Essence; the external appearance of these worlds will go on changing!" Her conviction held firm. Her inner flight to her Beloved was a frequent occurrence. The little one's surrender had become complete.

Sometimes Sudhamani saw Krishna walking along beside her. At other times, when she herself became inwardly identified with Krishna, she would feel like tearing all the pictures of gods and goddesses, including that of Krishna, off the wall. "These portraits are just paper and paint; they are not Krishna! I myself am Krishna!" The next moment her attitude would change, "No, I should not tear down these pictures; it was this portrait which helped me to attain Krishna. Everything is pervaded by Krishna, the Supreme Consciousness. Therefore, this portrait is also That!"

Beholding and realizing everything as Krishna marked the culmination of years of sacrifice and yearning. Now Sudhamani was seen embracing trees, kissing plants and small children as, wherever she turned, she saw the enchanting form of Lord Krishna. There was not even an infinitesimal point where He was absent.

Later, she said about this period,

"I used to look at Nature and see everything as Krishna. I could not even pluck a single flower, because I knew that it was also Krishna. When the breeze touched my body, I felt that it was Krishna caressing me. I was afraid to walk because I thought, 'Oh, I am stepping on Krishna!' Every particle of sand was Krishna for me. Now and then I strongly perceived myself to be Krishna. Gradually this became a natural state. I could no longer find any difference between myself and Krishna who dwelled in Vrindavan."

Thus Sudhamani became established in the Ocean of Pure Existence and Bliss and attained perfect peace of mind. However, her identity with the Supreme still remained unknown to the family and villagers. Though externally she looked like the same ordinary village girl, internally she was one with the Lord Krishna, the natural state of abiding as the One Reality.

Chapter Five

For the Good of the World

"All the Deities of the Hindu Pantheon, who represent the infinite aspects of the One Supreme Being, exist within us as well. A divine Incarnation can manifest any one of them for the good of the world by mere will. The Divine Mood of Krishna (Krishna Bhava) is the manifestation of the Purusha or Pure Consciousness aspect of the Absolute."

– Mata Amritanandamayi

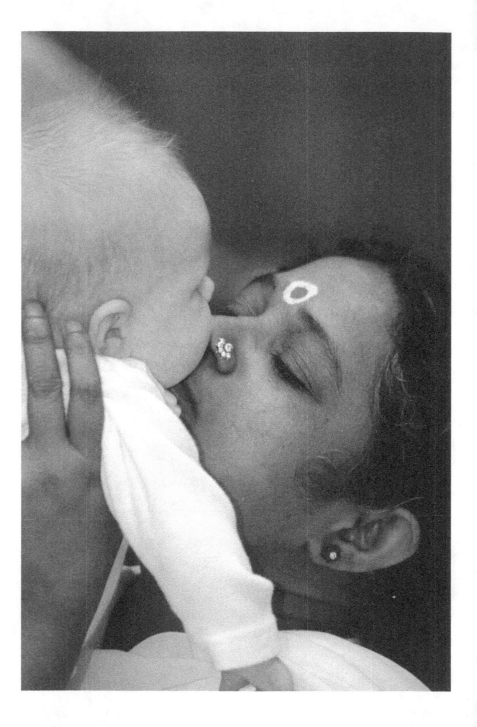

Vamsī vibhūṣita karāt navanīra dabhāt
pitāmbarāt aruna bimba phalā taroṣṭāt
purnēntu sundara mukhāt aravinda nētrāt
kṛṣṇāt param kimapi tatva maham na jāne

I know no Reality other than Sri Krishna whose hands
hold the flute, Who is beautiful like a fresh rain cloud,
Who wears yellow robes, Whose lips are red like an
aruna bimba fruit, Whose face is charming like the full
moon and Whose eyes are elongated like lotus petals

— Madhusudana Saraswati

Advent of Krishna Bhava

Young Sudhamani, whose entire being had found eternal
rest in the Supreme, now struggled to carry on with the
household chores as before. She tried hard to discharge
her duties, but, as we shall see, this was not what the Divine had
in store for her.

On a Wednesday evening in the month of September, 1975,
certain events occurred which would later mark the beginning
of a new chapter in the annals of India's spiritual history. Sudhamani had just finished collecting grass for the cows, and was
returning home about five in the afternoon, accompanied by her
younger brother, Satheesh. Carrying a big bundle of grass on her
head, she was in her usual sublime mood and the melody of a

devotional song was on her lips. As the two passed the entrance gate of the neighboring house on the northern side of Idamannel, Sudhamani came to an abrupt halt. She had overheard the final verses of the Srimad Bhagavatam being read aloud in the courtyard[19]. The reading had come to an end and the devotional singing was just beginning.

Sudhamani stood motionless, captured by the moment, and appeared to be intently listening to the singing. Suddenly her mood changed dramatically. The bundle of grass fell from her head as she ran to the spot and stood in the midst of the devotees gathered there. Overwhelmed with divine bliss, her inner identification with the Lord overflowed into her external being, transforming her features and movements into those of Sri Krishna Himself!

Stunned, the devotees believed that Sri Krishna had indeed come to them suddenly in the form of this village girl in order to bless them. Sudhamani asked one of the devotees to bring some water, which she then sprinkled on everyone as sacred water. News of Sudhamani's Divine Manifestation spread quickly, and soon a large crowd gathered. Some skeptics raised objections to the little one's sudden Divine Mood saying, "If you are really Lord Krishna, then you must show us proof through a miracle. Otherwise, how can we believe?" Instantly came the reply,

"An object which does not already exist cannot be brought into existence. All things are really only the projection of the mind. Having the Real Gem within you, why do you crave an imitation? Even though Pure Being is within you, ignorance is veiling it!"

---

[19] Every month the household of a man named Sri Narayanan from the next village would conduct the reading of this great epic which highlights the life and sportings of Lord Krishna.

Unable to grasp this sublime truth uttered by one established in Pure Being, they pressed her again and again to show a miracle. Sudhamani responded,

"I am not interested in making someone a believer by showing a miracle. My intention is not to show miracles. My goal is to inspire people with the desire for liberation through realisation of their Eternal Self. Miracles are illusory. They are not the essence of spirituality. Not only that, once a miracle is shown, you will demand to see one again and again. I am here not to create desire, but to remove it."

The skeptics insisted, "No, we won't ask again; show us a miracle once, we won't insist again!" At last Sudhamani conceded, "In order to inculcate faith in you, I will do it once, but never again approach me with such desires. Those who doubt, let them come to this same place on the day of the next Srimad Bhagavatam discourse."

When the next Bhagavatam discourse was held, a huge crowd had gathered inside and outside the house. The non believers even climbed trees and perched on rooftops, hoping to expose a fraud. Revealing her oneness with Krishna, Sudhamani told one of the doubters to bring a pitcher of water, which, as before, she sprinkled on the devotees as sacred water. Then she asked the same man to dip his fingers in the remaining water. To everyone's amazement the water had become pure milk! This was then distributed among the crowd as a holy offering from God. Then Sudhamani called another skeptic, asking him to dip his fingers in the pitcher. The milk in the pot had now turned into a sweet and fragrant pudding (panchamritam) made of milk, bananas, raw sugar, raisins, and rock sugar. All present raised a cry, "O God! O God!" and believed themselves to be truly in the Divine Presence of Lord Krishna. The panchamritam was distributed among more than a thousand people who had gathered, yet the pot remained full to the brim. Some people who were sitting at a distance near a small banyan tree at the seaside also received the sweet pudding, but still the vessel's contents did not diminish. A few skeptics, still not satisfied, declared the whole incident a feat of mesmerism, insisting that the panchamritam would vanish within a few seconds. Much to their disappointment, it did not vanish, and the sweet scent remained on everyone's hands for several days. This event greatly increased the faith of the villagers, who now all firmly believed in Sudhamani's divinity.

Referring to the advent of Krishna Bhava, Sudhamani subsequently explained,

"In the early days, I used to dance in bliss and move about alone, persisting in Krishna Bhava, but no one knew. One day I strongly felt the urge to be absorbed in the Supreme Being without returning. Then I heard a voice from within saying, 'Thousands and thousands of people in the world are steeped in misery. I have much for you to do, you who are one with Me.'"

It was after hearing this voice that Sudhamani manifested her inner identity with Lord Krishna to the villagers. Sudhamani continued,

"I was able to know everything concerning everyone. I was fully conscious that I, myself, was Krishna, not only during that particular time of manifestation, but at all other times as well. I did not feel, 'I am great'. When I saw people and knew their sufferings, I felt immense pity for them. I was conscious of devotees offering salutations to me and addressing me as 'Lord'. I could understand the sorrows of the devotees, even without being told."

From that time on, Sudhamani regularly revealed Krishna Bhava near a small banyan tree growing on the western side of Idamannel near the seashore path. Around the tree there were lovely flowering plants as well. A few years earlier the villagers had planned to construct a temple there. To inaugurate the temple site, some of the village youth had planted another banyan tree and lighted a sacred oil lamp.

Sugunanandan had encouraged the youths and had actively participated in their efforts. His elderly mother, Madhavi, often accompanied by Sudhamani, would come each evening, light the oil lamp and sing some sacred songs. A tiny hut, thatched with woven coconut leaves, had been built in front of the banyan tree, and portraits of Lord Krishna and Mother Kali had been installed inside[20].

Now several years later, this became the spot where Sudhamani revealed her identity with Lord Krishna. As the piece of land was public property, it was a convenient location for people to gather to participate in the auspicious Krishna Bhava. Lying horizontally on a slender branch of the banyan tree, Sudhamani would assume the posture of Anantasayana, Lord Vishnu reclining on the thousand-headed serpent, Ananta. By self-will her body would become as light as air at this time. This was a wonderful sight for the devotees.

This sacred spot became a veritable Vrindavan, the Abode of Sri Krishna, and the atmosphere was pervaded with devotional songs in praise of the Lord. Devotees began to flock to the place, not only for the auspicious darshan of Sri Krishna, but also to obtain relief from their problems. The devotees' distress would mysteriously vanish after they had unburdened their troubles to Sudhamani during the Krishna Bhava.

In those days, when people prayed for a solution to their problems, Sudhamani, as Krishna, would instruct them to light a piece of camphor and place the burning camphor on her protruding tongue. She would then swallow it along with the fire!

---

[20] This little shrine is located near the gravel road on the way to the oceanside from the ashram.

After the Bhava had ended, nobody could find a trace of a burn on her tongue. This practice also increased the faith of the people.

News of Krishna Bhava quickly spread, and people from Kerala and other parts of India began flocking to Parayakadavu. This marked the beginning of a pilgrimage to this holy place which has continued with ever increasing numbers of seekers to this day. Some people came asking for relief from disease, some sought freedom from material difficulties, others came out of curiosity, and some came out of devotion. But one thing they all discovered was that, after coming to Sudhamani, they found a solution for their problems.

One group of local skeptics began coming with the hope of exposing a fraud, which was how they perceived Sudhamani's Divine Mood. But the little one remained equipoised under all circumstances. She would later explain,

"During the Bhava, different kinds of people come to see me, some out of devotion, others for a solution to their worldly problems, and others for relief from diseases. I discard none. Can I reject them? Are they different from me? Are we not all beads strung on the one life thread? According to each one's level of thinking they see me. Both those who love me and those who hate me are the same to me."

During the first two Krishna Bhavas, Sugunanandan had been out of town on business. When he came to hear of the mysterious transformation of his daughter, he suspected it to be some undiagnosed disease. However, he decided to see the Krishna Bhava for himself before making a decision. Therefore, he arranged a Bhagavatam reading at Idamannel, and, on that day, Sudhamani again revealed her oneness with Sri Krishna. Having seen the Divine Mood of his daughter, who since birth had been full of surprises, Sugunanandan was wonderstruck and could not utter a word. From then on, Sugunanandan, who had always been an ardent devotee of Lord Krishna, participated in all the Bhava Darshans, which had become a regular event in this sacred coastal fishing area.

At this point, the parents still believed that Sudhamani's Divine Moods were only possessions of Lord Krishna and that her devotional practices were temporary aberrations that would stop one day. They waited for that day to come, so that they could give her in marriage. They cannot be blamed for their misconception, as they were not at all aware of Great Souls and their behaviour. Theirs was a simple view of God: His manifestations on earth were, in their mind, limited strictly to the idols of the gods and goddesses in the shrine rooms and temples. God was not to be found elsewhere, least of all in their eccentric daughter!

Notwithstanding their previous experiences, the parents again made arrangements for Sudhamani's marriage, and again Sudhamani fiercely threatened any prospective groom who was unfortunate enough to arrive at Idamannel. Finally, Sudhamani angrily warned her parents, "If you succeed in giving me in marriage, I will kill the man, and then come back to Idamannel!"

The parents, having bitterly failed to marry off Sudhamani, decided to seek the advice of a well-known astrologer[21], who lived in a distant place, and had never heard of Idamannel, Sudhamani or her Divine Mood. The parents were full of hope that at last they would circumvent her stubbornness. After consulting Sudhamani's horoscope, the astrologer turned to Sugunanandan, and said in a solemn tone, "This girl is a Mahatma (Great Soul or Saint)! If the marriage is not yet arranged, please do not make any further effort to do so. If the marriage has already taken place, call her back immediately. Otherwise you will have to face a great calamity; it will be the cause of great sorrow for you." The

---

[21] In India, marriages are traditionally arranged by the parents after an astrologer consults the son's or daughter's horoscope.

dejected father returned home with a heavy heart, and all plans for Sudhamani's marriage were dropped.

When people understood that Sudhamani's manifestation of Krishna Bhava was genuine, more and more of them came to receive her blessings. At the same time, some people came hoping to take advantage of Sudhamani's divine benevolence to further their selfish motives and to make money. One night, some people approached Sudhamani to see if she could be tempted by money. They offered her a large sum if she would show them some miracles. Sudhamani laughed out loud and affectionately told them,

"I have nothing to gain by showing miracles. My goal is not to gain fame and material prosperity by exhibiting miracles. There is an immense and inexhaustible wealth of divinity within us. Discarding that, why should one chase after the perishable and trivial wealth of the world? Selfless service to God and suffering humanity is my life's goal. I am here not to earn anything, but to renounce everything for the happiness of others."

Every day the number of devotees increased, as the wonderful experiences of those who had come to Sudhamani in Krishna Bhava inspired others also to take refuge in her. The seashore around the banyan tree came alive with devotional singing, and the villagers, forgetting their differences, gathered together to receive her blessings.

On one occasion, a huge crowd of devotees had gathered at the sacred banyan shrine during Krishna Bhava. Suddenly, dark menacing storm clouds gathered overhead, and a downpour quickly followed. As there was no shelter available nearby, the devotees simply stood waiting for the inevitable drenching. But to the amazement of all, no rain fell on the place where the devotees were standing, although it fell in torrents all around them!

During this period, a poisonous cobra often frightened people walking in the village, particularly at night. People frequently saw the cobra moving freely about, and everyone became afraid to walk along the seashore at night. Some of the villagers approached Sudhamani during Krishna Bhava to pray for a solution. Then one evening during the Divine Mood the dreaded serpent made an appearance. The crowd scattered, cowering at a distance. Sudhamani fearlessly caught hold of the cobra and touched its flicking tongue to her own! Then she released it. Never again were the villagers troubled by the venomous snake, and once more they were able to walk freely along the shore.

Once the 'Children of Mother Sea,' as the fisherfolk were known, were starving, because they had been unable to catch any fish for many days. They approached Sudhamani during Krishna Bhava and confided their misery to her. Giving them a tulasi leaf[22], she instructed them to have a young boy drop it into the sea at a particular spot and then to fish there. In order to test her, the fishermen did not act on her advice but approached her again during the next Darshan (audience). Before they could say a word, Sudhamani pointed out their mischief and once again offered them a tulasi leaf. Surprised and remorseful, they accepted the leaf and proceeded to the sea, but somehow they failed to drop it in the designated spot. Taking pity on them during the next Darshan, Sudhamani blissfully danced on the seashore and, in that way, bestowed her blessing. To the fishermen's great joy and relief, the next day a vast school of fish swam right up to the shore. Never before in the history of the village had there been such a bountiful catch. On two other occasions Sudhamani performed similar wonders in response to the sincere prayers of

---

[22] Tulasi is a variety of basil which is considered to be holy and sacred to Sri Krishna.

the fishermen. But this self-centred and desire-prompted devotion of the villagers did not win much favour or encouragement from Sudhamani.

Though Krishna Bhava was the external manifestation of Sudhamani's infinite spiritual power, which she expressed through the form of Krishna, her parents and most of the villagers believed that she was merely being possessed temporarily by Lord Krishna during the time of the Bhava. Her elder brother and parents also had the idea that she was suffering from schizophrenia or some other mental delusion. For her part, Sudhamani was willing to let them believe that. At this point, apparently she was content that the people were feeling devotion to God and relief from their worldly sufferings as a result of the Bhava Darshan. This divine drama was to unfold in its further stages and at the proper moment according to the needs of the people.

Conducting the Bhava Darshan near the seaside had its drawbacks, although it was true that the devotees could gather there freely. While some came out of reverence and devotion, a persistent group came to abuse and harass Sudhamani. Not only that, but the rapid increase in the number of devotees had given rise to some odd developments around the banyan tree. One self-motivated group of villagers had even formed an administrative board which promptly decided to install a locked box for monetary offerings for themselves. This was the forewarning of the formation of a troublesome alliance.

These occurrences made Sugunanandan very sad. One night he approached Sudhamani during the Krishna Bhava and expressed his concern, "It is painful for me to see You performing Bhava Darshan on this roadside. Also it is intolerable to hear nonbelievers poking fun at You. Besides, You are my daughter, and it breaks my heart to see You surrounded by all sorts of people in a public place." Saying this, he burst into tears.

Sudhamani replied, "In that case, give Me another place to receive My devotees. If there is no other place, that cowshed will suffice." Sugunanandan readily agreed, and arrangements were made to repair the cowshed. It was cemented, and a half-wall added down the middle to divide it into two sections. One side remained a cowshed, and the other side was prepared for the Bhava Darshan. All four sides were covered with woven palm leaves.

Soon the Bhava Darshan was shifted from the seaside banyan tree shrine to Idamannel, where it continues to the present day. During Krishna Bhava, Sudhamani stood now in the newly built shrine. While leaning on the half-wall, she would now and then reach over to put her hand on one of the cows which were standing on the other side.

One night during Krishna Bhava, Sudhamani called her father and told him,

"My devotees will come from far and wide. Many of the devotees will settle here permanently. You will have to face many obstacles, but do not be afraid. Endure everything. Do not take revenge against anyone. Do not be envious. Do not seek anything from anyone. Everything you need will come to you unasked. Always give part of what you receive in charity. In time, this place will become a great spiritual centre. The little one will travel around the world many times. Though you may have to suffer a lot in the near future, God will always bless you and provide for your needs. Your relatives and even the villagers will hate you and abuse you, but in time they will become your friends. Thousands of My devotees will become like your own children. From this day on, the little one is ever pure."

Once more, Sugunanandan was wonderstruck! His dark blue daughter, who had suffered countless beatings at his own hands, was going around the world?! Why, she had never been as far as Cape Comorin![23] Thousands of people were coming to Idamannel? Where on earth would they all stay? The house was tiny! And what was the meaning of her saying that the little one was ever pure?[24] Though these words left a deep impression in Sugunanandan's mind, at the time he dismissed them as crazy utterances. Only after years had passed did he realize the absolute truth of what his daughter had said to him that day.

Some of the local people found that their interests had suffered from the relocation of Krishna Bhava, and loudly protested saying, "We don't want a God who follows her father's wishes!" The devotees who used to sing at the banyan tree shrine now split into two groups. One group declared its opposition in the form of non cooperation, while the other group came to Idamannel to sing bhajans (devotional songs) during the Bhava Darshan as before. Exasperated by the loyal group of devotees, a group of villagers began coming to Idamannel with the sole intent to quarrel and cause trouble. They abused the bhajan singers openly, as they sang during the Bhava Darshan. This antagonistic group, consisting of both men and women, persisted until one day Sugunanandan became completely fed up. He and some other devotees chased them out of Idamannel, but this was only the beginning of the trouble.

The Rationalist Movement

Some of the truculent group were sons of the village landlords. They banded together to form an organization which they named "The Committee to Remove Blind Beliefs", also known

---

[23] Cape Comorin or Kanya Kumari is the southern tip of India, two hundred kilometers to the south of Parayakadavu.

[24] After Krishna Bhava began, Sudhamani never had her monthly period.

as "The Rationalist Movement." From thirteen coastal villages they managed to round up a thousand youths, who began their campaign to put an end to Sudhamani's Divine Mood.

The villagers had loved the virtuous and noble minded Sudhamani since her childhood, when she used to greet each morning with her enchanting singing to Krishna. Furthermore, they had unwavering devotion and faith in her Divine Mood, but Sugunanandan's unyielding nature aggravated the latent feelings of envy or enmity that some had. From the outset of Krishna Bhava, Sudhamani had warned her father during one Darshan not to quarrel with anyone or take revenge on anyone who opposed her. Not heeding her divine advice, Sugunanandan took some steps against the committee, which only intensified the enmity of the so-called rationalists.

They began by inventing slogans mocking Sudhamani. They then published notices filled with baseless and irrational criticism of her. Their vindictive campaign did not end there; their effort to defame Sudhamani and bring an end to Krishna Bhava had just begun. Their next step was to lodge a false petition with the police against her, stating that she was cheating people in the name of devotion! As a result of the petition, some police officers came to Idamannel to interrogate her. Wholly unperturbed, Sudhamani told the officers, "Please arrest me if you like, and take me to jail. Here, the family and villagers do not allow me to meditate. At least in jail I shall have solitude to meditate on God. If it is God's Will, let it be done." Having spoken, she stretched out her hands. The police officers were very much impressed to see her bold yet innocent way of addressing them and facing the situation. A few thought she must be crazy, but the others were charmed by her personality and felt sorry that such a Great Soul was being rudely scandalized and persecuted for nothing. These officers paid their homage and left Idamannel. The following song was composed by Sudhamani during the time of the false petition and police inquiry:

Bhagavane Bhagavane

Thou art compassionate to the devotees...
O Pure Consciousness!
Destroyer of all transgressions!
Are there only sinners in this world?

O Bhagavan! O Bhagavan![25]
Who is there to instruct in the righteous path?
The Essential Principles[26] *are only found*
Printed on the pages of books...

O Bhagavan! O Bhagavan!
What one sees is just
False costume and trumpery.
O Kanna, please protect and
Restore righteousness!

One evening at twilight while the devotional singing was going on, another police officer, who was not satisfied with the first investigation, came to Idamannel on the basis of some new complaint. To his surprise the atmosphere had a soothing effect on him and, unable to find anything offensive or amiss, he also left the place without uttering a word.

The miscreants still continued their efforts to put an end to Sudhamani's Divine Mood. They now turned to much more direct and aggressive tactics to achieve their desired end. Their next plan was to go to Idamannel in small groups during the Bhava Darshan and seize Sudhamani during the Divine Mood,

---

[25] Oh Lord! Oh Lord!
[26] This refers to the eternal spiritual truths stated in the Vedic Scriptures.

thus dishonouring her and at the same time making a sham of the Darshan. After catching hold of her, they intended to rough her up. These hooligans were convinced that their straightforward plan would succeed, as they prided themselves on their courage and strength. However, before the night was over they left Idamannel full of shame, as, for some inexplicable reason, not one among them dared to approach Sudhamani during the Divine Mood.

Undeterred, they now hired a black magician infamous for his deadly sorcery. He himself came to Idamannel and offered Sudhamani some so-called 'sacred ash', in which he had invoked malevolent forces. This ash was prepared from the charred body of a cobra and was known to be so powerful that its evil effects would cause death to the person to whom it was given. Even to receive such ash in one's hand was considered a bad omen which would bring about great disaster. Fully aware of the supposed consequences, Sudhamani took the ash and rubbed it on her body in front of the misguided man. She thought to herself, "If the body is to perish by this, let it be so. If it is God's Will, can anyone escape it?" The unscrupulous man waited a long time to witness the agonizing effects of his sorcery which never materialized. Finally, he had to leave, admitting utter defeat, as nothing unusual had occurred even after hours had passed.

Now desperate to finish off Sudhamani and her Divine Mood, the miscreants launched their most treacherous plan. During the Krishna Bhava they entered the temple and offered Sudhamani a glass of deadly, poison-laced milk. Sudhamani played her role impeccably, and, graciously smiling, drank the whole glass of milk without hesitation. The murderous enemies anxiously waited inside the shrine to see Sudhamani collapse in convulsions and die. To their bitter dismay, after a few moments Sudhamani turned in their direction, vomited the poisonous milk right in front of them, and continued to receive devotees as if nothing had happened. The rationalists fled and temporarily gave up their campaign against her. The other obstacle which Sudhamani continually faced was the attitude of her own family. Despite the incessant harassment which she received from her relations, Sudhamani's mind never wavered in its equanimity, tolerance and compassionate resolve to assuage the pain of the suffering, whether friend or enemy, family or foreigner.

The formation of the antagonistic organization and its evil intention to harm the innocent Sudhamani created great mental distress for Sugunanandan. During this period, it was Sudhamani's habit to spend her nights outdoors, meditating under the star-filled heavens. Since her childhood she had always held sacred the solitude and silence of the night, when she could commune with the Divine and dance blissfully in a God-intoxicated mood without interference.

Sugunanandan's fear for his daughter increased when he thought that her enemies might stealthily attack her while she sat meditating alone. Hence, one day he commanded, "Daughter, come sleep in the house!" Sudhamani firmly reassured her father, "I have no house of my own. I prefer to sleep outside. God is omnipresent. He is everywhere, outside and inside. So why should I worry? If someone comes to harm me, God will protect me."

As for Damayanti, when the Krishna Bhava began, she had faith in Krishna, but once the Bhava had ended, her abusive attitude toward her daughter persisted as before. She believed that Sudhamani was possessed by Krishna only during the time of the Bhava Darshan, and that otherwise she remained as usual her lowly servant and eccentric daughter. After the advent of Krishna Bhava, Damayanti had no choice but to exempt Sudhamani from her household responsibilities as, at any moment, her mind might soar into samadhi regardless of where she was. If she happened to be cooking or wading through the backwaters, this total absorption would put her in real danger.

As previously noted, Damayanti was very orthodox when it came to her daughter's conduct. She prohibited Sudhamani from talking to any devotees after the Darshan had ended, particularly to young men. If she did so, Damayanti severely chastised and beat her without hesitation. She still feared that her unusual behaviour would bring dishonour to the family name! Although Sudhamani was beyond all attachment and aversion, the parents mistook her for an ordinary girl with all human feelings, attractions, and weaknesses, except during the Bhava Darshan. We can only wonder how those who were closest to her were least able to recognize her constant abidance in God-Consciousness.

The most intractable member of the family was Subhagan, Sudhamani's elder brother. He could not accept his sister's manner of receiving devotees and was completely intolerant of her ecstatic devotional singing and dancing. Sudhamani, who was beyond all duality, would receive men and women, children and elders, in the same equal manner. This infuriated Subhagan who, besides being an atheist, fiercely believed that women were inferior to men and should remain silent and unseen. He considered his sister a schizophrenic, and tried his utmost to create obstacles for her.

One day, he intentionally broke the oil lamp which the devotees kept lit in the temple during Krishna Bhava. Those who arrived that night for the Darshan felt very disheartened to see the broken lamp, as there was no other to replace it. Seeing their unhappy faces, Sudhamani asked some devotees to fetch a few seashells. When they were brought, she asked that wicks be placed in them and lit, although no oil was available. Then the impossible happened. Not only did the wicks light, but they burned throughout the night until the Krishna Bhava was over, without even a drop of oil! When asked how this could have happened, Sudhamani simply said, "The lamps burnt through the night because of the sankalpa²⁷ of the devotees." On the next Bhava Darshan day, a devotee who was unaware of the broken oil lamp and the subsequent incident, made an offering of oil lamps for the shrine. Responding to the queries of devotees, he explained that he had had a dream in which he was instructed to bring them.

Some of the villagers who arrogantly ridiculed Sudhamani had to face great disasters in life. The following is one such incident.

Sudhamani was returning home one day after visiting a nearby house. By the side of the path stood a group of villagers. As she passed them, Sudhamani overheard one of them teasing her. A wealthy villager was telling another man in a loud voice, "See this girl, she is crazy. She is always singing, dancing and pretending to be Krishna. What nonsense! This is a case of emotional hysteria. If her father would just give her in marriage, her disease would be cured." Hearing his critical remarks, his friends burst into laughter. He continued egotistically, "If her father needs a dowry, I am ready to give him credit for two thousand rupees to marry the girl off. I must tell him today!"

Sudhamani didn't utter a word. Reaching home, she ran to the family shrine room, locking herself inside. Sitting there she began pouring her heart out to Krishna, "O Krishna, don't You hear what they are saying? They call me crazy! They know nothing of Your beauty and instead would bind me to their own self-centred way of life. O Krishna, Protector of those who seek Your refuge, have You too abandoned me? If that is so, then who will worship You, seeing my desperate condition? Is this the reward for the tears I have shed thinking only of You? Is this love and devotion of mine merely the raving of a crazy girl? All these days You have been my only comfort. In the blue sky I see Your smiling face, in the waves I see Your dancing form. The morning

---

²⁷ A pure resolve.

doves' song is Your divine flute playing ! O Krishna, Krishna..."
Thus praying she began sobbing and collapsed on the floor.

Meanwhile, the wealthy man who had teased Sudhamani, was busy readying his fishing boats and nets for the day's fishing. Gathering his workers, he pushed off into the sea. That day they had an exceptionally good catch and all were rejoicing as they rowed back to shore.

On the way back, some of the workers who loved and worshipped Sudhamani remarked to the boat owner, "You know, it was not right to tease the innocent child the way you did today." The owner sneeringly retorted, "And what if I did? See what happened because I teased her: we got a bigger catch than usual!"

The devotees were tongue-tied and hung their heads. The boat was nearing the shore when suddenly the owner cried, "Hey, why don't we go to Neendakara[28]? There we will get a good price for our catch. In Parayakadavu the prices are very low." Agreeing, they steered the boat to Neendakara. They had almost reached the destination when suddenly the sea became rough. In no time huge waves rose up and dashed against the wooden hull. The boat full of fish, nets, and men was hurled about violently by gigantic waves. All efforts of the fishermen to control the craft were useless. The boat began sinking. The next instant, seized by an enormous wave, it was dashed on the rocks and broken in pieces. The day's catch was lost, one of the proud owner's best boats was destroyed, and his fishing nets lay torn on the rocks. Only their lives had been spared. With great difficulty, the fishermen managed to swim to shore.

A totally unexpected disaster had befallen the arrogant boat owner. Now it was his turn to walk along the shore with his head hanging. Crushed, he collapsed in the sand, unable to bear his great loss. The workers, who were admirers of Sudhamani, whispered to each other, "See the result of God's anger! He was just boasting

---

[28] A town in Kerala well known for its fish markets.

about his good fortune after teasing the little one. Now see what has happened!" Another worker devotee chimed in, "He left the shores of Parayakadavu after saying that the little one was suffering from hysteria, and even boasted that he would give two thousand rupees to marry her off. Now let us see where he will borrow that money!" Altogether that day he had lost seventy-five thousand rupees. The workers took a bus home, and the news flashed everywhere.

In those days, Sudhamani would sometimes suddenly become playful like a three year old child, and would make playful mischief with the devotees who had come for Krishna Bhava. When the Darshan was over, she would creep about stealthily and approach sleeping devotees. Sometimes she would tie the end of one woman's sari to the hair of another. At others, Sudhamani would pour a handful of sand on the men who used to sleep with wide open mouths. Harshan, Sudhamani's lame elder cousin, had great respect and love for her. If he happened to be sleeping somewhere after the Darshan had finished, Sudhamani would seek him out. Catching hold of him by the legs, she would drag him about, laughing. It was a big joke for him as well, and all the devotees would burst into laughter seeing Sudhamani's childlike sports. Subhagan never liked such actions of his sister and would scold her for her peculiar behaviour. How could he, who knew nothing at all of spirituality, understand the exalted state of Sudhamani?

Regarding her strange behaviour, Sudhamani said,

"My mind is always shooting up to merge with the Absolute. I am always trying to bring it down; only then can I serve the suffering and mingle with the devotees. That is why I play such games, to keep the mind engaged in the world of the devotees, though without attachment."

Chapter Six

As a Child of the Divine Mother

"As noble aspirations clearly manifested themselves in my mind, the Divine Mother, with bright, gentle hands, caressed my head. With bowed head, I told Mother that my life is dedicated to Her."

— Mata Amritanandamayi

Sivastvam gurustvanca saktistvamēva
tvamēvasi māta pitā ca tvamēva
Tvamēvasi vidyā tvamēvāsi bandhur
gatirmmē matirddēvi sarvam tvamēva

O Devi, verily You are Siva, You alone are the Teacher,
You alone are the Supreme Energy, You alone are the
Mother, You alone are the Father.
For me, knowledge, relatives, sustenance and
Intelligence, all are You.

– Devi Bhujangam

Devotion

The unique charm and beauty of Bhakti (devotion) are indescribable. A true devotee's sincere desire is to remain a devotee forever. He wishes to attain neither heaven nor liberation. For him, devotion is his life, and the Lord is his All-in-all. The devotee experiences the highest joy in singing the glory of the Lord. That is why the Bhakti Shastras[29] declare:

Devotion alone is the fruit of devotion.
In its intrinsic nature this divine love
Is Immortal Bliss.

---

[29] Devotional scriptures like *Narada Bhakti Sutras*.

Even the great saint, Suka, though he was thoroughly established in Supreme Consciousness, experienced ineffable exaltation in singing the glories of the Lord. Such is the bliss derived from pure devotion.

Sudhamani, who was fully established in the consciousness of Krishna, still had an unquenchable thirst to enjoy the bliss of Supreme Devotion, Para Bhakti. But her complete identification with Lord Krishna made it impossible for her either to meditate on His Form or to be immersed in His thought. Thus her prayers ceased flowing to Krishna, and her Krishna sadhana came to an end.

Then Sudhamani had a vision which brought about a great change in her manifestation of God and her service to the world. This unexpected vision opened the way for Sudhamani's Devi sadhana, her passionate quest to realize the Divine as the Mother of the Universe. As she sat alone one day in a room of the house, her eyes open, her mind was turned inwards, absorbed in the Self. Suddenly, right in front of her appeared a globe of brilliant light, reddish as the setting sun and, at the same time, as soothing as the moon. The globe of light neither rested on the earth nor hung in the sky. It was revolving. Against the background of this radiant, yet cooling disc of light, emerged the enchanting form of Devi, the Divine Mother, with a beautiful crown adorning Her head. Thrilled by this heart-capturing vision of Devi, Sudhamani cried out, "O Krishna, Mother has come! Please take me to Her, I want to embrace Her!" At once, Sudhamani perceived Krishna lifting her. He ascended with her above the clouds, where she beheld strange sights: lofty hills, vast dense forests, blue snakes and terrifying caves. But the little one could not find Devi anywhere. Like a small child, Sudhamani called out, "I want to see my Mother! Where is my Mother?" and began crying.

The exquisite vision of the Great Enchantress had disappeared from her sight, but became firmly fixed in Sudhamani's heart forever. She remained immersed in an enraptured state for a long time. From that moment on, she cherished the desire to behold again the benign smile and compassionate face of the Divine Mother. Sudhamani, who had beheld the Divine Form of Sri Krishna countless times, was ravished by the ineffable radiance of Devi. Her heart rushed after Devi, and her only desire now was to embrace the Divine Mother, sit on the Mother's lap and kiss the Mother's cheek.

Thus Sudhamani, who had never meditated on any form other than that of Sri Krishna, who had strongly believed that there was no Deity higher than Sri Krishna, now dedicated her entire being to realize the Divine as the Universal Mother, Adi Parashakti[30]. Except for the time she spent in Krishna Bhava, she plunged into deep contemplation of the resplendent form of the Divine Mother. The fire of longing for Her Vision burned in Sudhamani's heart without ceasing. Previously, her household duties had required that she remain functional in the mundane world, but now this fetter had been broken and she became completely lost to this gross plane of existence. It became a struggle for her even to maintain the most minimal care of her body. For months she subsisted only on tulasi leaves and water.

Sometimes when Sudhamani came out of deep meditation, she would cry aloud, "Amma! Amma! Where have You gone? Did You come that day only to abandon me? Please have mercy on this child of Yours and again reveal Your exquisitely gracious Form! O Mother, if I am deserving, make me one with You. I cannot bear this agony of separation! O Mother of the Universe, why

---

[30] The Primal Supreme Energy, the Creatrix, the feminine counterpart of the masculine 'Shiva' or Pure Consciousness.

are You indifferent to the heartbroken call of this child? Please embrace me, do take me on Your lap!"

Kannunir kondu

I shall wash Thy Feet with my tears.
O Katyayani, forsake me not.
How many days must I wait, my Mother,
For the Vision of Thy Form?

Though Thou delayest in giving what I want,
My mind is satisfied because of Thy Maya.
Wilt Thou allow me to offer
A red flower at Thy Feet?

Through this forlorn path
I wander in the hope of finding Thee.
Is there any kindness in Thy hard heart,
Tell me, O Beloved of Siva?

Just as Sudhamani had perceived everything to be pervaded by Krishna at the end of her Krishna sadhana, she now felt the Divine Presence of Devi in everything. Even the breeze was the breath of Devi. The innocent one roamed about talking to plants, trees, birds and animals. She felt the earth to be her Mother, and she rolled in the sand calling, "Amma, Amma! Where are You? Where are You not?"

One day after finishing her meditation, Sudhamani came out of the tiny shrine room. She was suddenly overwhelmed with the feeling that she was a small child, and that Nature was the Divine Mother. In that mood she crawled like a baby on all fours to the base of a coconut tree. Sitting there shedding tears, she pleaded, "Mother... my Mother... why are You hiding from my sight? I know that You are hiding in this tree. You are in these plants,

You are living in these animals, these birds! The earth is nothing but You. O Mother, how You conceal Yourself in the ocean waves and in the cooling breeze! O Mother, my elusive Mother!..." The next moment she embraced the coconut tree, feeling that it was the Divine Mother.

Sometimes Sudhamani lay down, but not to rest, as she had no fondness for sensuous pleasure. While lying on the bare ground, she would gaze endlessly at the infinite sky, the silvery clouds, the shining sun, the glittering stars, the soothing moon. When dark storm clouds gathered overhead, Sudhamani no longer saw Sri Krishna in them, but imagined the long, cascading, curly hair of the Divine Mother. Each object suspended in the infinite heavens became a sign of the presence of Devi. As she lay under the sky, she never slept, but remained in a state of tear-filled supplication to the Supreme Mother of the Universe.

Referring to those days, Sudhamani later recalled, "While walking I used to repeat the Divine Name with every step. I took each step only after chanting the mantra. Should I forget to chant the mantra while taking a step, immediately I stepped backwards. Having withdrawn the step, I would repeat the mantra. Only then would I proceed. If I happened to be engaged in any external activity, I used to decide beforehand to chant the mantra a certain number of times before finishing the task. While bathing in the river, before plunging into the water, I used to resolve to chant the mantra a certain number of times before coming to the surface. I never had a Guru, nor was I ever initiated by anyone and given a particular mantra. The mantra which I used to chant was 'Amma, Amma'."

There is a scriptural injunction which states, "Actions naturally subside in the state of supreme devotion." This is clearly evident in the case of Sudhamani. In the morning she used to begin to brush her teeth, but the next moment her mind would vanish in the single thought of the Divine Mother. This state of focused concentration would deepen and continue for hours at a time. Her attempts to take a bath usually met with little success. Upon entering the bathroom, she would realize she had forgotten to bring a towel. After fetching the towel, she would notice she had also come without soap. Discouraged, she would exclaim, "O Mother, how much time is wasted just trying to take a bath! Instead, let my mind be fixed on You! To forget You even for a moment creates agonizing pain in my heart..." Abandoning altogether the idea of taking a bath, she would sit in the bathroom merged in samadhi. Hours would pass before somebody would discover her sitting there, deeply absorbed in meditation. A bucket of water poured over her head to rouse her sufficed finally for her bath! If she failed to respond, she was shaken violently, or simply carried into the house.

In the area along the coast there were no proper toilets. Each family erected a small scaffold over the backwaters, enclosing the frame with woven palm leaves. As there was no flooring, one had to perch on a board in order to perform one's nature calls. Many times while Sudhamani sat in such a latrine, she would tumble into the backwaters, having lost her external awareness.

Immersed in meditation on the Divine Mother, Sudhamani would sit for long hours. Before beginning, she used to make an inner resolve: 'I must sit for this much time.' Then she would give a command to the body, "Sit here, body." She would tell Devi, "Don't play Your tricks on me. Keep them to Yourself. If You do not allow me to sit and meditate, I won't let You go!" If any external disturbance impinged on her awareness, she would bite Devi and pull Her hair, until she realised that she was biting her own body and tearing out her own hair.

One day, Sudhamani was unable to sit for the chosen length of time, as she felt someone violently shaking her body, and the sensation disturbed her. Thinking, "This is Her trick! Why is She not allowing me to sit?" she suddenly opened her eyes, ran from the shrine room, and returned a moment later with a wooden pestle, intending to threaten Devi. Raising the pestle, the little one shouted "Today I will...", then the next moment she realised her senselessness. "What! To beat Devi? Is it right? Is it possible?" She dropped the pestle and resumed her meditation.

Sudhamani would not waste even a second without remembering the Divine Mother. If someone happened to talk to her, she imagined the person to be Devi. The person would continue talking until perceiving that the little one had mysteriously slipped off to another world. If she realised that a moment had passed without having remembered Devi, Sudhamani would be very distressed and confess, "O Mother, so much time was wasted!" To make up for the lost time, she would increase the length of her meditation that day. If she happened to miss a meditation, she would pace the ground the entire night, repeating the mantra and sincerely praying, "O Mother, what is the use of this life if I am unable to meditate on You? Without You there is only Maya waiting to devour me. O Mother, please give me strength! Grant me Your Vision! Dissolve me in Your eternal Self!"

Most of all, Sudhamani liked to meditate by the oceanside in the silent hours of the night. For her the crashing waves resounded with the sacred syllable, 'Aum'. The vast, deep blue heavens, sparkling with countless stars, reflected the limitless divinity of the Mother. There, in a moment, her mind turned inward to abide spontaneously in the Self.

If Sugunanandan were to search for his daughter on those nights, he would become very agitated when he was unable to find her in the house or yard. Eventually his search took him to the sea, where he would find her absorbed in deep meditation, sitting like an immovable rock. Some of the villagers, mistaking the purpose of Sudhamani's late night visits to the shore, began to spread unkind rumours about her. When these reached the ears of Sugunanandan, he strictly forbade his daughter from going to the sea at night.

These incidents, which characterize the early phase of Sudhamani's Devi sadhana, only served to convince her family more fully of her insanity. These high states of pure devotion were far beyond the reach of an ordinary person's imagination. Sometimes Sudhamani would sob like a small child, calling out to an imperceptible Being; at other times she would clap her hands and laugh aloud, then roll on the ground or try to kiss the ripples on the water, calling out "Amma, Amma". It is little wonder that the little one's flight of the alone to the Alone was mistaken for madness. Even the devotees who visited her during Krishna Bhava utterly failed to comprehend this passionate quest of Sudhamani's for attaining oneness with the Divine Mother.

It is ironic that although her family considered her to be one gone mad, they never tried to discover the cause or cure. Instead, they persisted in their habit of taunting and tormenting her, especially her elder brother Subhagan. Their treatment finally became so inhumane, that Sudhamani resolved to put an end to her life by jumping into the ocean. She cried, beseeching the Divine Mother, "Am I such a wicked girl? Why do the family members persist in their cruelty? People love only those who are charming. I cannot see pure love anywhere in this world. O darling Mother, I feel everything to be an illusion. O Mother, are You not the Protector of Your devotees? Am I not Your child? Have You also forsaken me? If so, then why should I carry this body? It is a burden for me as well as others. Accept Your child, O Mother Sea!" With a determined mind Sudhamani ran toward the ocean, yet, when about to jump, she saw the vast sea to be Devi Herself. Unable to keep her mind on the physical plane, she entered into samadhi and fell unconscious on the sand.

Harshan, Sudhamani's cousin and devotee, had overheard her parting prayer as she ran from Idamannel. He followed her in haste, having understood her intention. Finding her unconscious by the water's edge, he reverently carried her back to Idamannel, thanking God that he had found her still alive.

Many villagers sympathized with Sudhamani, although some of them also considered her mad. They would remark to one another, "See how pitiful her condition is! Poor girl! Nobody looks after her; even her parents have discarded her. When she was healthy and normal she toiled day and night for them, but now they are not even interested in caring for her. Is she not their daughter?"

Some of the women who lived in the neighbourhood took pity on Sudhamani and began to serve her lovingly. These women had had deep admiration for her since her childhood. They were now devotees of the Krishna Bhava and recognized Sudhamani's spiritual splendour and all-embracing love. Somehow, they had a vague understanding of her sublime spiritual states. Whenever they could, they helped her or rescued her from danger.

Chellamma and her daughter, Vatsala, lived on the plot of land which lay in front of Idamannel. Vatsala considered Sudhamani her close friend and had boundless love for her. Living so close to Idamannel, she and her mother often noticed the little one's unconscious tumbles into the backwaters. Immediately, they would fish her out of the water, dry her off, and dress her in clean clothes.

Pushpavathi and her husband, Bhaskaran, were both ardent devotees. She loved Sudhamani as her own daughter and felt sad to see how the family tormented her. Two sisters, Rema and Rati, who also lived near Idamannel, held the little one very dear to their hearts. Another loyal friend , Aisha, Sudhamani's cousin on her aunt's side, was extremely fond of the kind and affectionate Sudhamani. These ladies were the ones who were blessed to serve Sudhamani during her days of intense tapas[31]. Often when Sudhamani became oblivious to the surroundings, one of the ladies would find her lying in muddy water or in a dirty place. If they could not revive her, they would carry her in their arms to their own house. As if she were a small child, they would brush her teeth, give her a hot bath, dress her in fresh clothes, and feed her with their own hands.

As before, Subhagan remained always antagonistic to Sudhamani and her Divine Mood. Several times he pressed her to discontinue the Krishna Bhava, as he still considered it a shameful display which would bring dishonour to the family name. As his demands were ignored, he decided to take more drastic steps.

One day after the Bhava Darshan, Sudhamani was about to enter the house, when she found her way obstructed by Subhagan, who stood menacingly in the doorway. He shouted at her, "Do not enter this house! You will be permitted to come inside only after you stop this shameful singing and dancing!" Taking his words to be Divine Command, Sudhamani walked away without murmuring a word and sat down in the front yard. Loudly Subhagan prohibited her from sitting there either. Upon this, Sudhamani took a handful of sand and gave it to Subhagan saying, "If it is yours, please count this sand!"

Thenceforth, she lived outdoors, which she was happy to do. The sky overhead became her roof, the earth her bed, the moon her lamp, the sea breeze her fan. These austere conditions only served to intensify her renunciation and determination to realize the Divine Mother. Raising her hands above her head with tears rolling down her cheeks like a small child appealing to its mother,

---

[31] Severe austerities.

Sudhamani would cry out aloud, "Amma, Amma... have You left me here to die with longing for Your Vision? The days are passing one by one. Still I have no peace of mind without beholding Your enchanting Form. All my hopes lie in You. Will You also forsake me? Do You not see my desperate condition?" During this period, Sudhamani wrote the following songs:

Bhaktavalsale Devi

O Devi, O Ambika, Beauty Personified,
O Thou who art affectionate
Toward devotees,
May Thou dwell here in order to end
The sufferings of the devotees...
Thou art everything, powerful enough
To end my misery, the tap root of all...

Thou standest as the Empress of all beings,
Thou art the world and its Protector as well...

Believing this, I am praising Thee with Devotion.
O Goddess of the Universe, I desire to see Thee...

For how many days have I been desiring to see Thee...
I am praising Thee without losing even a Moment...

Did I commit some error or hast Thou no mind to end
my sorrow?

Or perhaps Thou wishest that my inner self be
Burnt to ash. I am getting confused; I know nothing...

Will the truth that I keep in my heart that all
The children are equal to the Mother become false?

In order to end my misery I will request
A little of the nectar of Thy Grace pouring
From the glance of Thy holy eyes...

I will fall at Thy Feet in order to see
Thy gracious face and beg for the boon of
The fulfilment of Life...

Oru tuli sneham

O Mother, for the satisfaction of my life
Give a drop of Thy Love to my dry, burning heart.
Why o why dost Thou put burning fire
To fertilize this scorched creeper?

Bursting out crying, how many
Hot tears have I offered before Thee?
Dost Thou not hear my heart throbbing
And agony coming out as suppressed sighs?

Let not the fire enter and dance
Through the forest of sandalwood trees.
Let not this fire of sorrow show its strength
And burst forth like shattering tiles...

O Devi, chanting the Name 'Durga, Durga'
My mind has forgotten all other paths.
O my Durga, I want neither heaven nor liberation.
I want only pure devotion to Thee...

Her tapas became so intense that Sudhamani's body became extremely hot, as if she were standing on burning coals. The heat became so unbearable that she could hardly wear clothes. Seeking relief from the burning sensation, she would roll in the muddy sand of the backwaters. Sometimes she stood submerged in the backwaters for hours in deep meditation.

Sincere and ardent devotees of Sudhamani used to invite her to their homes during times of special worship. They believed that her presence would bestow spiritual splendour and power on all who attended. These families used to come to Idamannel to take Sudhamani to their house by bus. Sometimes Sudhamani would become God-intoxicated while waiting at the bus station. Forgetting the external world, she rolled on the ground and burst into blissful peals of laughter. Of course people could not comprehend her state and would gather around her, watching in astonishment. Others would tease and rebuke her, calling her a crazy girl. Children used to stand around her ridiculing her, but such treatment was lost on Sudhamani. What taunting words could reach the world where she was revelling? What harassment could taint the innocent girl's intoxicated mood of Divine Bliss?

In her deep anguish of separation from the Divine Mother Sudhamani would sometimes cry and scream aloud. Small children would gather around her on such occasions begging, "Elder sister, don't cry! Are you suffering from a headache?" Eventually they, too, came to understand that she was crying to see Devi. During these uncontrollable outbursts, one of her younger sisters would stand before her, assuming the pose of Devi, wearing a sari and cascading hair. In great joy, Sudhamani would run to embrace her. If she should notice any beautiful girl when she was in this mood, she would run to her enthralled. Embracing and kissing her, she saw only Devi.

Seeing his daughter's utter neglect of her body and taking pity on her, Sugunanandan tried several times to build a thatched shelter to protect her from the rain and sun. As she was lying or sitting merged in meditation, her parents would take the opportunity to construct a shade above her. Coming back to a state of normal awareness and seeing what her parents were doing, she would move away from the place saying, "This also will become a cause for sorrow. For how many days will you be able to keep it here? If you go away somewhere, who will maintain it? Unaffected by anything, let me endure heat, cold and rain, and thereby transcend them."

In those days of intense yearning for the Divine Mother, Sudhamani assumed the nature of a two year old child, the child of the Divine Mother. Her identification with this attitude of child to Mother was so complete that many of her actions can be understood only in the light of this fact. One day, coming out of meditation, Sudhamani felt very hungry and thirsty. Just then, she saw Pushpavathi of the neighboring house breast feeding her baby. Straightaway Sudhamani went to her, displaced the suckling baby, and lay in the woman's lap for nourishment. Instead of feeling awkward about this unexpected act of Sudhamani's, Pushpavathi overflowed with motherly feelings for her. Similar incidents occurred several times, until Pushpavathi realised it was safer to feed her baby out of sight of the innocent-minded Sudhamani.

One day Sudhamani was lying unconscious in the mud and sand near the backwaters. Some devotees who found her felt appalled to see her lying there with her nostrils, eyes, ears and hair full of dirt and sand. The incessant stream of tears had left visible streaks on her dark blue cheeks. The devotees informed Sugunanandan of her pitiful condition, but he ignored their plea. Dismayed by his indifference, they carried her into the house where they were unable to arouse her. They cleaned the dirt from her body, unwittingly laid her on her elder brother's cot, and left her to rest comfortably.

Returning home, Subhagan found Sudhamani lying on his cot. He flew into a rage and began shaking the cot violently. He became like a madman, screaming, "Who put this wretch on my bed? Who put this wretch on my bed?" The bed broke into several pieces, but Sudhamani lay there in the middle of the debris, lost to the world. Later, when she came to know about the incident and her close brush with danger, she simply said, "Whatever happens is God's Will." The very next Darshan, much to everyone's amazement, a devotee who was a carpenter, and who was totally unaware of the previous day's incident, presented a cot, a table and chairs to Sudhamani. When he was asked about this, he said that he had had a dream in which Krishna had appeared and told him to bring all those things for the little one.

Chapter Seven

Far Better Than Man

"Human beings are not the only ones with the capacity for speech. Animals, birds and plants have this power but we do not have the capability to understand. One who has the Vision of the Self knows all these things."

– Mata Amritanandamayi

Ahimsā pratiṣṭāyām tat
sannidhau vairatyāgaha

On being established in harmlessness,
all beings coming near him cease to be hostile.

— Patanjali Yoga Sutras, sadhana padam, verse 35

While Sudhamani was living outdoors, dogs, cats, cows, goats, snakes, squirrels, pigeons, parrots and eagles all sought her company and became her intimate friends. This phase of her sadhana demonstrates the power of love, untainted by attraction and aversion, to bring harmony among animals who are otherwise natural enemies. At a time when her own relations had abandoned her and were vehemently opposed to her spiritual life, these animals stood by her and rendered loyal service. Their behaviour clearly revealed that they seemed to understand Sudhamani far better than human beings. In those days, Sudhamani could not eat anything from her own house, as she was extremely sensitive to food prepared by worldly people. The only food she could eat was what had been prepared while mantras were chanted. One day, as she came out of the temple after meditation, she felt very hungry and thirsty. In front of the temple was a family cow, which she perceived instantly as a gift from God. Playing the role of a calf, she drank directly from its udders, thereby quenching her thirst and hunger, while the cow kept its legs in a convenient position. From that day on, the cow lay in front of the temple each day until Sudhamani emerged from her meditation. Before feeding her, the cow would refuse to graze or to feed its own calf! Sugunanandan tried several times to force the cow to move away from the spot where it waited for Sudhamani. He pulled the cow's tail and poured buckets of water over it, but it would not budge from in front of the temple.

On some days, someone brought milk from the neighbourhood for the little one to drink. However, the milk was not pure; it had been mixed with water. When Sudhamani drank it, she vomited, and the one who had sent the adulterated milk was fated to suffer for the act. For that reason, Sudhamani decided to eat and drink only what was provided by God.

Another extraordinary incident occurred about this time. In the village of Bhandaraturuttu , where Sudhamani's grandmother lived some six kilometres to the south, Sudhamani's uncle, Ratnadasan ,untied the cows from the cowshed as usual, to bring them to the front yard where he fed and bathed them. Suddenly one of the cows turned abruptly and trotted toward the ocean, where it took a sharp turn toward the north. The cow ran rapidly up the beach, as Ratnadasan struggled to catch up with her. Finally the cow turned into Sudhamani's village, and ran directly to Idamannel, where it had never been. Heading straight for the place where Sudhamani was sitting in meditation, the cow began gently nuzzling and licking her, as if to express love to an old friend. As Sudhamani remained still deeply immersed, the cow lay down nearby, intently watching her, as if waiting for her to finish her meditation. After some time Sudhamani opened her eyes and, noticing the vaguely familiar cow, walked over to it. At that moment the cow raised a back leg, inviting her to drink its milk. Sudhamani drank from the udder, as her uncle shook his head in disbelief.

What mysterious power had inspired the cow to visit Sudhamani? Though she had tended that cow during her brief stay at her grandmother's house many years ago, does that explain the animal's unprecedented behaviour?

When Sudhamani sat outdoors in meditation, snakes sometimes appeared and coiled around her body, as if to bring her awareness back to the external world. One day, following some harassment from her family, Sudhamani left the grounds of Idamannel. A lady from the neighbourhood encountered her as she walked, consoled her, and led the little one to the peace of her own house. Sudhamani promptly entered the family shrine room and began pouring her heart out to the Divine Mother. It was then that she composed the following song:

Manasa vacha

*Through my mind, speech and actions I am
Remembering You incessantly.
Why then are You delaying to show
Your mercy to me, beloved Mother?*

*Years have passed but still my mind has no peace.
O darling Mother, please grant me a little relief...*

*My mind sways like a boat caught in a storm.
O Mother, give me a little peace of mind
Lest I become a lunatic...*

*I am tired Mother; it is unbearable.
I don't want such a life. I can't stand
Your tests. O Mother, I can't endure it!*

*I am a miserable destitute.
I have none but You Mother.
Please stop Your tests,
Extend Your hand and pull me up...*

Suddenly, her mood changed and she fell into a fit of divine madness. Crying and rolling on the ground, she began tearing at her clothes. The next moment she burst into laughter, still rolling uncontrollably. The family watched in concerned amazement and had no idea how to calm her. At this point, a large snake appeared in the doorway and crawled directly onto Sudhamani's body. The family stared, horrified, as the snake began licking the unconscious girl's face with its flicking tongue. This went on for some minutes and immediately had a soothing effect on Sudhamani. As her mind slowly returned to a normal plane of consciousness, the snake crawled off her body and disappeared. It seemed to the family that the snake knew the exact remedy to restore Sudhamani's external awareness and deftly administered to her needs.

Any visitor to Idamannel soon notices that many kinds of birds make their home there. Sudhamani used to love the parrots especially, as they were dear to the Goddess. Sometimes when she prayed, "O Mother, won't You come near me?", a flock of parrots would fly to her and settle on the ground nearby. One day a devotee presented her with a parrot, which always played around Sudhamani, who never caged it. One day Sudhamani was thinking, "Oh, what a terrible, cruel world it is! Not even an iota of truth or righteousness exists anywhere. People are deceitful, and the world has become filled with sinners. It seems there is nobody to show the correct path to humanity." As tears flowed down her cheeks, she remained in an introspective mood for a long time. At one point, Sudhamani noticed her parrot was standing in front of her also shedding tears, as if it were suffering from some pain. Her intense agony had moved the bird as well.

Besides the parrot, two pigeons also kept her company. Whenever she sang to the Divine Mother, the three birds would hop before her, dancing joyfully and spreading their wings.

From a big tree on the Idamannel property, an eagle's nest[32] once fell to the ground, and two fledglings tumbled out, dazed and vulnerable. Some mischievous children threw stones at the tiny birds trying to kill them, but Sudhamani quickly rescued them. She carefully nursed them for a few weeks until they were strong enough to fly; then she set them free. These two Garudas always returned at the beginning of each Krishna Bhava and would sit on the top of the shrine for a long time. They were a great source of attraction for the devotees, as the Garuda bird was the vehicle of Lord Vishnu. The mysterious connection which the two birds maintained with Sudhamani not only added splendour to the Darshan, but also increased the devotees' faith in her divine nature.

During the period of Devi sadhana, whenever Sudhamani lost consciousness, weeping to see the Divine Mother, these two birds would appear from the sky to sit beside her as if to protect her. Some of the ladies from the neighbourhood watched with wonder as the two birds, gazing at Sudhamani's agonized face, also clearly shed tears with her.

One day soon after meditation, Sudhamani felt terribly hungry. One of the two Garudas immediately flew toward the ocean and returned a few minutes later with a fish in its beak. The eagle put the fish on the lap of Sudhamani, who gratefully took it and ate it raw. When Damayanti discovered this, she used to wait for the Garuda to come with its daily offering. As soon as the bird dropped the fish, Damayanti swooped in to grab it, so that she could cook it for her daughter. During the sadhana period when Sudhamani was intent to realize Krishna, she had stopped eating fish, as even the smell would make her vomit. But now the fish

---

[32] The eagle is called 'Garuda' in India. Garuda is the vehicle of Lord Vishnu of whom Sri Krishna is an incarnation.

brought by the Garuda was food sent by God , so she gladly ate it. The daily practice of the Garuda continued for some time.

Another animal which seemed attuned to Sudhamani was a cat. During the Bhava Darshan the cat would enter the temple and walk around Sudhamani as if doing pradakshina[33]. It would then sit near her for a long time with its eyes closed and seemed to the devotees to be meditating. Once someone tried to get rid of the cat by taking it across the river, but the next day it returned and stayed by Sudhamani's side.

A unique black and white dog also showed remarkable faithfulness. When Sudhamani cried so much to Devi that she fell unconscious in her prayers, the dog would rub against her and lick her face and limbs in order to revive her. When Sudhamani seemed to be leaving the Idamannel property, the dog tugged at her skirt and barked in protest to prevent her departure. Often he would bring a food packet in his mouth and lay it before her to eat. The dog wouldn't eat even a grain of rice from whatever he had brought as an offering. At night the dog would sleep near Sudhamani, who would use him as a pillow when she lay down to gaze at the sky.

One night the little one was meditating while sitting on the banks of the backwaters. She was steeped in samadhi and a thick blanket of mosquitoes covered her body. Sugunanandan called her, but no reply came. When he began roughly shaking her body, he found that she had become as light as a twig. "Her whole body looked lifeless, but as I had found her in that condition many times, I wasn't worried," Sugunanandan later explained. As he sat by his daughter, the black and white dog appeared, fiercely barking. Within a few minutes, Sudhamani opened her eyes and came back to her normal awareness. Animals seemed to have a

---

[33] Circumambulating a holy object while keeping it to one's right.

greater ability than humans to draw Sudhamani's attention when she became enraptured in another realm.

Sometimes the intense love of the dog made Sudhamani think that it was the Divine Mother Herself. Forgetting everything she would embrace and kiss the dog, calling aloud, "My Mother, my Mother...!"

One day while meditating, Sudhamani felt extremely agitated. Immediately she rose from her seat and walked hastily toward the village. The black and white dog had fallen into the hands of a dog catcher; it was howling and crying piteously, but it was not acting at all vicious. Unable to escape from the catcher's sling, it was dragging its paws as its captor struggled to haul it away. Some of the village girls, who were friends and admirers of Sudhamani, recognized the dog as her faithful companion and begged the dog catcher to free it. They even promised a bribe if he would let the dog go. At this moment Sudhamani arrived. The dog looked pitifully at her and began shedding tears! This was too much for the dog catcher; he had no choice but to set the dog free.

Another dog from the neighbourhood also had intense love for Sudhamani. One day during the dog's pregnancy, it came to the side of the temple and stood expectantly waiting. When Sudhamani came out of the shrine after meditation, she found it standing on the temple verandah. It did not step in, but placed its forelegs on the edge of the temple floor and howled in a peculiar way as if it were in pain. Sudhamani embraced and kissed the dog asking, "What happened daughter, what happened?" Thereupon, the creature stepped down from the temple verandah, lay down on the sand, and breathed her last breath.

Whenever somebody prostrated before Sudhamani, the black and white dog used to stretch its forelegs and bow its head down before her. When she danced in devotional ecstasy, the dog jumped around her as if joining in the ecstatic dance. When the sacred conch was blown during the twilight worship each evening, the dog would howl in a peculiar way, closely imitating the sound of the conch.

One day Sudhamani had an intense feeling that her friend, the black and white dog, would die afflicted by rabies. Shortly thereafter the animal did contract rabies and died as she had foreseen, though without much suffering. When Sudhamani was asked if she were dejected to lose her loyal companion, she said, "I am not at all sad about his death. Even though he died, he will come to me. Therefore, why should I be sad?" Later, she commented that the dog's soul had reincarnated near Idamannel, but would reveal no further details.

Regarding a goat which had great love for her, Sudhamani once remarked, "On account of a disease of her udders, the goat was struggling for life. She was about to die, when I saw her agony and sat down near her, lost in prayer and meditation. When I opened my eyes I beheld the poor animal approaching me, crawling on her knees. Placing her head on my lap, she quietly died, gazing at my face. Her love was pure indeed."

Some years later recollecting all these incidents she expressed these thoughts: "How blissful were those days! Strangely enough, those animals could understand my feelings and act on them. If I cried, they also would join me in crying. If I sang, they would dance in front of me. When I lost my external consciousness they would crawl over my body. All the traits of various animals can be found in human beings. When one gets rid of all attachment and aversion and attains equal vision, then even hostile animals become friendly in one's presence."

Chapter Eight

Dazzling Like a Million Suns

"Smiling She (Devi) became a Divine Effulgence and merged in me. My mind blossomed, bathed in the many-hued Light of Divinity, and the events of millions of years gone by rose up within me. Thenceforth, seeing nothing as separate from my own Self, a single Unity, and merging in the Universal Mother, I renounced all sense of enjoyment."

– Mata Amritanandamayi

Driśā drāghīyasā dara dalita nīlotpala rucā
davīyamsam dīnam snapaya kripayā mām api shive

Anenāyam dhanyo bhavati na ca te hānir
iyatāvane vā harmlye vā sama kara nipāto himakaraha

*O Spouse of Siva! Wilt Thou graciously bathe even me,
who stands helpless at a far off distance, with Thy far-
reaching glance, beautiful as the slightly blossomed blue
lily. This mortal will derive the greatest good of existence
from Thy action. By such action, no loss is, after all,
sustained by Thee. The snow-beamed Moon sheds the
same lustre on a forest as on a mansion.*

– Saundarya Lahari, verse 57

Placing her absolute faith in the Divine Mother, Sudhamani swam in the Ocean of Immortal Love. For her,
the whole atmosphere above, below, right and left, was
surcharged with Her Divine Presence. The breeze was the loving caress of the Mother. The trees, vines and flowers were all
Devi and hence worthy of Sudhamani's undifferentiated worship. Gazing at the sky, seeing what we know not, the little one
would be overcome with uncontrollable fits of tears and laughter
which subsided only when she fell unconscious to the sand. The
imploring prayers of this orphaned child to her vanished Mother
echoed in the air of Idamannel day and night. It was at this level
of Realisation, seeing all of Nature as being the Divine Mother
only, that she wrote the following song:

Shrishtiyum niye

Creation and Creator art Thou,
Thou art Energy and Truth,
O Goddess, O Goddess, O Goddess!

Creator of the Cosmos art Thou,
And Thou art the beginning and end...
The Essence of the individual soul art Thou,
and Thou art the five elements as well...

Attended mostly by the now familiar clan of animals, Sudhamani was neither sleeping nor eating. She never made contact with other people unless they first approached her, and even a basic task such as brushing her teeth was ignored by her soaring mind. When she did eat, she sometimes consumed discarded tea leaves, cow dung, glass pieces or human excreta; she was unable to notice any difference between delicious food and all of these. What words are there to describe that state which our mind and intellect are incapable of grasping?

No longer could the little one contain her agony, and her prayers poured forth incessantly to the Divine Mother,

"O Mother, my heart is being torn by this pain of separation! Why does Your heart not melt seeing this endless stream of tears? O Mother, many Great Souls have adored You and thereby attained Your Vision and became eternally one with You. O Darling Mother! Please open the doors of Your compassionate heart to this humble servant of Yours! I am suffocating like one who is drowning. If You are not willing to come to me, then please put an end to my life. Let that sword with which You behead the cruel and unrighteous fall on my head as well. At least, let me be blessed by the touch of Your sword! What sense is there in keeping this useless body which is a heavy burden for me?"

Sudhamani's anguish became extreme, her prayers exhausted. In her own words,

"Each and every pore of my body was wide-open with yearning, each atom of my body was vibrating with the sacred mantra, my entire being was rushing toward the Divine Mother in a torrential stream..."

In unspeakable agony she cried out,

"O Mother... here is Your child about to die, drowning in unfathomable distress... this heart is breaking... these limbs are faltering... I am convulsing like a fish thrown on the shore... O Mother... You have no kindness towards me... I have nothing left to offer You except the last breath of my life..."

Her voice became choked. Her breathing stopped completely. Sudhamani fell unconscious. The Will of the Mother designates the moment. The Divine Enchantress of the Universe, the Omniscient, the Omnipresent, the Omnipotent Being, the Ancient, Primal Creatrix, the Divine Mother, appeared before Sudhamani in a living form dazzling like a thousand suns. Sudhamani's heart overflowed in a tidal wave of unspeakable love and bliss. The Divine Mother benignly smiled, and, becoming a Pure Effulgence, merged in Sudhamani.

The divine event is best described in Sudhamani's own composition 'Ananda Veethi' or 'The Path of Bliss' , in which she has tried to make intelligible that mystical union which is beyond words :

Ananda vithi

Once upon a time, my soul was dancing
In delight through the Path of Bliss.
At that time, all the inner foes such as
Attraction and aversion ran away, hiding
Themselves in the innermost recesses of my mind.

Forgetting myself, I merged in a golden dream
Which arose within me. As noble aspirations
Clearly manifested themselves in my mind,
The Divine Mother, with bright, gentle hands,
Caressed my head. With bowed head, I told
Mother that my life is dedicated to Her.

Smiling, She became a Divine Effulgence
And merged in me. My mind blossomed,
Bathed in the many-hued Light of Divinity
And the events of millions of years gone by
Rose up within me. Thenceforth,
Seeing nothing as separate from my own Self
A single Unity, and merging in the Divine Mother,
I renounced all sense of enjoyment.

Mother told me to ask the people
To fulfil their human birth.
Therefore, I proclaim to the whole world
The sublime Truth that She uttered,
"Oh man, merge in your Self!"

Thousands and thousands of yogis
Have taken birth in India and
Lived the principles visualized by the
Great Sages of the unknown past.
To remove the sorrow of humanity,
How many naked truths there are!

Today I tremble with bliss
Recollecting Mother's words,
"Oh my darling, come to Me,
Leaving all other works.
You are always Mine."

O Pure Consciousness,
O Embodiment of Truth,
I will heed Your words.
O Mother, why are You late in coming?
Why did You give this birth?
I know nothing, O Mother,
Please forgive my mistakes.

At this point Sudhamani developed a strong aversion to the visible world. She would dig big holes to hide in, so as to escape from the diverse world and sensuous-minded people. She spent her days and nights enjoying the perennial Bliss of God-Realisation and avoided all human company. If anyone had considered her mad before, they were firmly convinced of her insanity now. Who could conceive of the plane of consciousness in which she was established? Though internally Sudhamani had crossed the threshold into the Absolute, externally she was the same crazy Sudhamani who was possessed three nights a week by Krishna as far as the family and villagers were concerned. The only recent change, if they had noticed any at all, was that instead of rolling in the sand, she was now digging big holes.

Advent of the Devi Bhava

One day Sudhamani heard a voice from within her say,
"My child, I dwell in the heart of all beings and have no fixed abode. Your birth is not for merely enjoying the unalloyed Bliss of the Self but for comforting suffering humanity. Henceforth, worship Me in the hearts of all beings and relieve them of the sufferings of worldly existence..."

It was after this inner call that Sudhamani began manifesting Devi Bhava, the Mood of the Divine Mother, in addition to the Krishna Bhava. At these times, she revealed her oneness with the Divine Mother, though, for the devotees, she had now merely become possessed by Devi as well as Krishna. The following incident marks the advent of Devi Bhava.

Only six months had passed since the beginning of Krishna Bhava Darshan. It was now late in 1975. One night as the Krishna Bhava was going on and the devotees were entering the temple one by one, an unexpected incident changed the whole atmosphere.

As usual, some devotees were singing bhajans outside the shrine room on the verandah. Sudhamani was manifesting her inner identification with the Sri Krishna aspect of the Supreme and was receiving the devotees joyfully. An enchanting smile lit up Her bright face, and the devotees were delighting in the Divine Presence. At that moment, a devotee entered the small temple completely distraught. Apparently, he had been severely harassed by one of the antagonistic villagers[34]. Unable to bear the sharp remarks, he burst into tears and appealed to Krishna to find some remedy for the situation.

Without warning, the gracious smile vanished. Sudhamani's entire facial expression changed and became fierce, as if the final dissolution had come. Her eyes looked like two smouldering iron balls. Burning with anger, they seemed to emit shooting flames. Her fingers were holding the Devi mudra[35]. All present both inside and outside the temple were shocked to hear boisterous laughter issuing from her whole being. They had never heard such laughter in their lives. Seeing the sudden change in Sudhamani, those standing in the temple began trembling out of fear. Some

---

[34] The miscreants were still in operation and would stand along the roadside where the devotees would pass and make cutting remarks. Not only the villagers but also Sudhamani's own father and brother would indulge in this. They would even try to discourage the devotees from remaining until the end of the Darshan.
[35] A divine gesture associated with the Divine Mother.

scholars who were present began loudly chanting peace mantras and devotional songs in praise of the Divine Mother, while some others performed the ceremony of Aarati[36]. After much prayer and chanting of various mantras, she became calm and peaceful, but the Bhava had been transformed from that of Krishna to that of Devi.

Sudhamani later confided, "Seeing the distress of that devotee, I felt like destroying all the unrighteous people who persist in ridiculing the devotees. Unknowingly, the Devi of fierce nature[37] manifested to grant refuge to the persecuted." Thenceforth, in addition to Krishna Bhava, the Holy Mother, as we will call her now, regularly gave Darshan to the devotees as Devi.

The Holy Mother was the embodiment of Universal Love. Those virtues obvious since early childhood such as the urge to love, help and serve people, fully unfolded. The Mother accepted the worldly and the spiritual, the illiterate and the educated, the rich and the poor, the sick and the healthy with the same equal tenderness and compassion. Patiently listening to all the problems which they came to unburden, she would adapt her counsel to the nature and maturity of each one. According to each one's need, she would guide and comfort them in all their difficulties.

Soon after the beginning of Devi Bhava Darshan, there occurred certain changes in Mother. During her Devi sadhana, she was generally aloof and uncommunicative. All her time was devoted to prayer and meditation on the form of the Divine Mother. If her parents or brother abused her physically or verbally, she kept silent. Now she became more daring, and even her facial expression changed. Her nature became fearless and unyielding when it came to dealing with her parents and brother over the issues of the Bhava Darshan and her association with the devotees

---

[36] The waving of burning camphor in before the Deity as a form of worship.
[37] Kali Mata.

in particular. She now began mingling more with the devotees and instructing them spiritually. This marked the beginning of the Mother's spiritual mission.

My Own Formless Self

"From that day onwards[38] I could see nothing as different from my own Formless Self wherein the entire universe exists as a tiny bubble..."

In this pithy utterance, the Holy Mother conveys a wealth of insight. Although established in the ultimate state of God-Realisation, the Mother performed additional sadhana to demonstrate that all the different forms of gods and goddesses are facets of the same non-dual Reality. Having attained perfect control over the mind, she found that she could identify herself with any aspect of the Divine which she chose by her own will. Mother has narrated various experiences which she had while performing these sadhanas:

"At the end of sadhana one day, I felt that a large canine tooth was coming out of my mouth. Simultaneously, I heard a terrific humming sound. I perceived the form of Devi with large canine teeth, a long protruding tongue, thick black curly hair, reddish bulging eyes and dark blue in colour[39]. I thought, 'Quick! Escape! Devi is coming to kill me!' I was about to run away. Suddenly I realised that I myself am Devi. The humming sound also was being produced by me. The next moment I found that I was holding Devi's veena[40]. I had Her crown on my head and I

---

[38] Referring to her experience of the Divine Mother.

[39] A description of Kali Mata.

[40] A stringed instrument always seen held in the lap of Saraswati, the Goddess of Knowledge.

was wearing the Mother's nose ring. After a couple of minutes I thought, 'What is this? How have I become Devi? Maybe this is a trick played by the Divine Mother to obstruct my sadhana.' So I thought, 'Let me meditate on Siva and see what happens,' but the moment I began meditating on Lord Siva's form, I became Him, matted hair, snakes on my neck and coiled on my upper arms. I thought, 'Maybe Siva is also testing me,' so I stopped meditating on His form. Now I fixed my heart and soul on Lord Ganesha, the remover of obstacles. Immediately my being changed to that of Ganesha, an elephant's face with a long trunk, a pair of tusks with one half broken, and so on. Whichever form of god or goddess I contemplated, I became. Then I heard a voice from within, 'You are not different from them. They have all merged in you long ago. Then why should you call all these gods and goddesses?"

Thenceforth, the Holy Mother's meditation on God with form naturally subsided. The all-pervasive sacred syllable 'OM' sprang forth from within the Her, and her whole being was forever merged in That. Even then, to set an example, she would sit and meditate. When asked about this, the Holy Mother explained, "During meditation, Mother approaches all the children, especially those who are intensely thinking of Mother or those who are suffering."

A similar incident occurs in the great epic, Srimad Bhagavatam. One day, when the renowned sage, Narada, visited Dwaraka, the Abode of Sri Krishna, he found the Lord sitting in deep meditation. Narada reverentially bowed to the Lord and asked, "O Lord, on whom are You meditating ?" The Lord smilingly replied, "I am meditating upon my devotees."

Although the little one had become "Mother" in the eyes of many, she remained Sudhamani to her family. Her natural abidance in the Supreme Self was far too subtle for her parents and elder brother to understand. They continued to doubt and misinterpret her behaviour as schizophrenia. They feared that her contact with the devotees would result in her deviating from the path of morality and thus bring disrepute to the family. Her brother Subhagan was especially fanatical in his aggression against the Mother, and his behaviour toward her became violent. One day, Subhagan and a few of his cousins called the Mother to a relative's house under a false pretext. When she arrived, they locked her in a room and one of her cousins began threatening her, suddenly pulling out a long knife which he had hidden in his clothing. Subhagan announced, "This behaviour of yours has gone too far! You are bound to spoil the family name. Since you cannot stop mixing freely with all sorts of people and persist in your singing and dancing, it is better that you die." He was enraged to hear the Mother laugh and retort, "I am not at all afraid of death. The body must meet its end sooner or later, but it is impossible for you to kill the Self. Now that you are determined to put an end to my physical existence, I will express a last wish. You are obliged to fulfil it. Let me meditate for a while, and then you may kill me while I am in meditation."

Hearing her daring answer, they became still more infuriated. One among them exclaimed, "Who are you to command us? Are we here to kill you or not kill you according to your wish?" Mother smiled and boldly retorted, "It seems that nobody but God alone can put an end to my life!" Another of the cousins shouted, "God! Who is your God?" Though they verbally threatened the Holy Mother, none of them was courageous enough to do anything to her after hearing her bold reply and seeing her unperturbed. Suddenly the cousin who had brandished the knife jumped forward and pressed the knife against her chest as if to stab her. But he could not make another move, as he was immediately stricken by an excruciating pain in his own chest at the exact point where he had pressed the knife against the Holy Mother's.

He himself fell to the floor in agony. Seeing this, the others in the room were filled with dread. At this moment Damayanti arrived, having seen Sudhamani leaving with Subhagan and his cousins. Hearing the uproar, she began pounding on the door, shouting. When the door was opened, Damayanti took the Holy Mother by the hand and led her home, taking the path by the shore. On the way back to Idamannel, the Mother told Damayanti, "Your people are dishonoured by me. This ocean is my Mother as well. She will accept me happily with outstretched arms. I am going to Her lap." Hearing her words, Damayanti became mentally unbalanced. She began screaming, "Don't say that, daughter! Don't say like that, daughter! During Krishna Bhava, Bhagavan told me that if you happen to commit suicide, all my children will go insane..." Succeeding in dissuading the Holy Mother, she took her back to Idamannel.

The episode does not end here. The cousin who had raised the knife against the Mother to stab her was taken in pain to the hospital. Though provided with excellent medical treatment, he finally died, continuously vomiting blood. As his disease was in its acute stages, the Holy Mother visited him in the hospital. She lovingly consoled him and fed him with her own hands. He was deeply repentant toward her for his grave mistake, and burst into tears experiencing her compassion and forgiveness.

The Holy Mother had no enmity toward her cousin who had attempted to murder her, nor had she made any resolve to avenge his evil act. He simply suffered the fruit of his action. The Mother explained,

"Just as human beings have intense love for Mother, numerous subtle beings love her as well. If somebody attempts to harm Mother, Mother does not react. Mother faces such a person without any excitement and does not even think any harmful thought regarding him who acts out of ignorance. But these subtle beings get angry and take revenge. Do you understand how this is? Suppose someone's mother is attacked by a man. Do the children sit back indifferent? Even if their mother tries to stop them, they find that man and take revenge."

Transcending the limitations of worldly existence, the Holy Mother would receive devotees without distinction of caste, creed, class or gender. In the eyes of ignorant nonbelievers, the equal vision and broad-mindedness of the Holy Mother was just the manifest symptom of a mental aberration. The miscreants continued to enter the temple during the Bhava Darshan to question the Mother antagonistically. Though the Mother remained unaffected and calm, Sugunanandan became very depressed by their insolent remarks. Furthermore, although all his attempts to arrange the marriage of his daughter had ended in failure, he still could not completely let go of this idea. He now began to feel the Bhava Darshan was a great impediment to the fulfilment of his wish. He joined Subhagan in his firm belief that the Darshan was a shameful thing. Something else also worried him. His daughter's body would become stone-hard after the Bhava and only hours of strong massage would return it to normal.

Sugunanandan's mind was resolved to join Subhagan to somehow put an end to the Bhava Darshan. Entering the temple during the next Devi Bhava , Sugunanandan told the Holy Mother, "Devi should go away from the little one's body. Here we don't need this Bhava Darshan anymore. We want to give her in marriage. I want my daughter back!"[41]

The Holy Mother addressed him as stepfather[42] and asked, "Is she your daughter?" Already agitated, he became more furious

---

[41] It should be remembered that as far as her family was concerned, the Holy Mother was possessed three nights a week by Krishna and Devi, and the rest of the time she was a crazy girl.

[42] Since she was young she had accepted only God as her real Mother and Father and thus everybody else was her stepmother and stepfather.

hearing himself addressed that way and angrily retorted, "Yes! She is my daughter. Do gods and goddesses have stepfathers? I want my daughter back!"

The Holy Mother calmly replied, "If I give back your daughter, she will be nothing but a corpse and will soon be decomposing. You will have to bury her, not marry her." Not being in the mood to listen, Sugunanandan demanded, "Let the Goddess go back to Her own place! I want my child back!"

The Mother said, "If so, here is your daughter. Take her!" Instantly the Mother fell to the temple floor. Within a few moments her body became stiff and her heartbeat stopped. Though her eyes were wide open, there was no sign of life to be seen. She was dead.

A great wailing arose. All those who had come for the Darshan became overwhelmed with grief. Damayanti and her other daughters fainted on the ground. The news flashed that Devi had taken away Sudhamani's life because of some error committed by Sugunanandan. Everyone accused him of being the cause of the untimely death of the Mother.

Oil lamps were lit around the body. Even Nature became silent in that moment. Some of the devotees burst into tears, others blabbered like idiots with sudden uncontrollable emotion. Others sat solemnly near the body, testing to see if there were any breath coming from the Mother, by holding their hands near her nostrils. Nothing. A doctor checked her pulse. She was dead. It was a terrible moment.

Coming to realize the horror of the situation caused by his indiscriminate action, and unable to bear the excruciating pain in his heart, Sugunanandan also fell unconscious. A mournful silence reigned. Thinking that the impossible had truly happened, all hope of reviving her was given up. Eight ominous hours dragged by. Regaining his consciousness only to confront the dreadful scene, Sugunanandan cried aloud his prayer to the Divine Mother, "O Devi! I beg You, forgive me for speaking words which I uttered in extreme ignorance! Please bring my daughter back to life! Forgive my fault! Never again will I repeat this despicable action!" Imploring, he fell on the ground, weeping uncontrollably in full prostration before the temple.

Suddenly one among the devotees noticed faint signs of movement in the Holy Mother's body. With soaring hope, the devotees watched her as their tears of sorrow were transformed into tears of joy. The Mother came back to life, but in Krishna Bhava! Addressing Sugunanandan, who was an ardent devotee of Krishna, she told him, "Without Shakti[43] there can be no Krishna!"

This incident brought about a great change in the father's attitude toward God and his daughter. From that time on, he left her to do as she liked and never again attempted to arrange a marriage for her. Later, the Mother remarked about this particular incident,

"He was adamant about getting his daughter back from Devi. But if she had really been their daughter, they would have had the power to bring her back to life as well. That they could not do. At the most, this body is theirs. When he demanded his child back, this body was given."

---

[43] The feminine aspect of the Cosmic Energy personified in the form of Devi.

Chapter Nine

The Sword of Truth

"Children, even when a man is cutting a tree down from its root, it gives him shade. A spiritual aspirant should be like this. Only he who prays even for the welfare of those who torment him can become a spiritual person. The spiritual aspirant's greatest weapon is the sword of Truth."

– Mata Amritanandamayi

Durvrtta vrtta samanam tava dēvi sīlam
rūpam tadhaitadavi cintyamatulya manyaih

Vīryam ca hantr hrtadēvaparākramānām
vairisvapi prākatitaiva dayā tvayēdham

*O Devi, Your nature is to subdue the conduct of the
wicked; this Your peerless beauty is inconceivable for
others; Your power destroys those who have robbed the
gods of their prowess, and You have thus manifested
Your compassion even towards the enemies.*

– Devi Mahatmyam, chapter 4, verse 21

It seems that all Great Souls must endure the persecution of
the mediocre minded. However, the Great Ones seem to
thrive on it, as every obstacle thrown in their path adds to
their glory. The lives of Sri Krishna, Sri Rama, Jesus Christ and
Buddha offer abundant illustration of this fact. The Holy Mother's
life is also a magnificent example. Three years had now passed.
By 1978 the number of devotees was growing rapidly, and people
were flocking to Idamannel from all parts of India for the auspicious Darshan of the Holy Mother. As her admirers increased,
the miscreants intensified their evil campaign, but no worldly
power could obstruct the spiritual mission of the Holy Mother.

At this time, certain bad omens were seen which presaged
an impending catastrophe at Idamannel. Subhagan was not at
all put off by the ill consequences of his attempt to have his sister
murdered in cold blood. He now became more openly arrogant
and hostile towards the Holy Mother. He tried to impose his own

selfish ideas on the whole family. Even they were afraid to oppose him because of his volatile, hot-tempered nature. The increasing number of devotees and the unabated slander of the rationalists set his mind on fire with restlessness. He began accosting devotees coming for the Bhava Darshan and severely abusing them hoping to dissuade them from partaking in the Darshan.

At this juncture, either due to fate or as a result of his vile actions bearing fruit, Subhagan became afflicted with the terrible disease elephantiasis. Symptoms of this disease appeared on both his hands and legs. Although he underwent various medical treatments, none had a curative effect. The thought that he had become terminally ill plagued him constantly. He became severely depressed and developed suicidal tendencies. Several times he expressed his mental anguish to his close friends. He developed insomnia as a result and resorted to taking sleeping pills. The cumulative effect of his physical and emotional afflictions took its toll and gradually Subhagan lost his mental balance.

One day the Holy Mother called Damayanti and told her, "It seems that brother Subhagan is nearing the end of his life span. As a solution you can take a vow of silence, but certain obstacles can be seen which will try to break your vow. Therefore, be careful when you take the vow." Adhering to the Mother's words, Damayanti observed a vow of silence one day. However, when it was halfway over, it so happened that a cow broke its rope and started running from their cowshed. Damayanti completely forgot her vow and shouted, "There goes the cow! Catch it!" The family took this as a bad omen, especially as Damayanti had been forewarned by the Mother to attend her vow with care. This inauspicious occurrence filled the family with fear and anxiety.

One day Subhagan, in a fit of fury, severely harassed a Muslim woman who had come to Idamannel for the Bhava Darshan. Unable to bear Subhagan's vicious remarks, the lady rushed to the temple, burst into tears and began beating her head against the threshold of the shrine room. She was crying out, "O Mother... O Mother... is this the fate of those who come to see You?"

Hearing the Muslim woman's distraught cries, the Mother's radiant and smiling face underwent an immediate transformation. With a terrifying appearance, she stood up from the sacred seat holding a trident in one hand and a sword in the other. In a solemn and deep tone the Mother said, "Whoever has caused this undue grief to this devotee will die after seven days."

When the Mother's prediction reached the ears of Sugunanandan, he rushed to the temple seeking forgiveness for his son's grievous behaviour. He pleaded to the Mother to spare Subhagan's life and take his instead. Mother calmly told, "I never punish anybody. If I am abused or harassed I don't care at all. But when a devotee suffers such abuse even God will not forgive. Each one must enjoy the fruit of one's actions. There is no other way."

Seven days had passed. It was nearly midnight on June 2, 1978 when Subhagan, who had been informed of the Mother's prediction, committed suicide by hanging. He had written a suicide note giving the reason as unbearable stress caused by his incurable disease. Subhagan's suicide created chaos and distress at Idamannel house. The miscreants immediately seized this opportunity to strengthen their anti-propaganda campaign against the Holy Mother. They began spreading fabricated versions of Subhagan's death. They accused Sugunanandan, who loved his eldest son like his own life, of murdering Subhagan.

For all their effort, the miscreants were unable to gain any ground with their unrighteous accusation as there was ample evidence that the death was a suicide. Besides the suicide note in his own handwriting, Subhagan had also sent letters to some of his friends and relatives informing them of his intention. The postmortem report also verified the death as suicide. Thus, the question of legal action did not arise.

Subhagan's suicide caused a stir among the relatives. They openly expressed their hatred and noncooperation by completely ignoring the whole family as if it never existed. The family was no longer invited to attend or participate in public functions, festivals, marriage ceremonies or religious rites and rituals. All the relatives abandoned them. The relatives would come to visit the house next door but would not even look in the direction of Idamannel. If the relatives came to the seashore near Idamannel to perform rites for the ancestors, they would quit the place immediately after they had made the offering. This treatment was very hard on the family and only added additional weight to their already heavy hearts.

Sixteen days after Subhagan's death when the Bhava Darshan was resumed, Sugunanandan approached the Holy Mother with a heavy heart. He complained that the Mother had not saved his dear son from a horrible death and burst into tears. Consoling him, the Mother said, "Do not worry. Your deceased son will again take birth as a devotee in this same house after three years." After a few years the eldest daughter, Kasturi was married. When she conceived her first child, the Holy Mother named the child 'Siva' while it was still in the womb. As the Mother had given a male name, the family was convinced that the child would be a boy. The child was in fact a boy. After his birth the Mother once told, "For the three years since Subhagan died, his soul has been around this Ashram atmosphere. Having heard the devotional singing and Vedic mantras, he was again given a birth as 'Siva' in this same house." Now Sivan is an intelligent young boy. Since his infancy he always chants the sacred syllable 'OM' and sits in meditation without being asked.

The Return of The Rationalists

After the beginning of the Devi Bhava, the rationalists became more arrogant and antagonistic. They now began using the news media to try and mislead people into thinking that the Holy Mother was a lunatic and that the Bhava Darshan was a fraud. However, the greater their efforts were to defame the Mother, the greater too their failures. Their persistence was really a wonder!

One night, the miscreants decided to try again their old but unsuccessful tactic of catching hold of the Mother during the Darshan to humiliate her and thus make a mockery of Godly power. Two of the rowdier members of their group appeared on the scene, fully drunk and eager to create trouble in the shrine room. They joined the other devotees in the queue in order to enter.

At that time, the Mother was already seated for the Devi Bhava and told some of the devotees who were sitting near her in the shrine, "Just watch, Mother will show you a good joke now." With these words, she looked directly at the drunkards and cast an enchanting smile at them. By this time, they had reached the doorway of the shrine room but the one who was standing in front became unable to move as if he was paralysed. He could not make another step and stood there frozen for a couple of minutes. His cohort who was immediately behind him became infuriated at this and asked in a harsh voice why he was not entering the temple. "Can't you see how many people are already standing inside the temple ahead of me!" he retorted. The other man shouted, "You are just standing like a lot of wood since a long time! Have you also been hypnotized by this girl?" This sharp verbal exchange escalated into a fierce fight between the two rowdies while they left Idamannel as had already been foreseen by the Holy Mother.

As previously mentioned, in those days some amongst the householder devotees used to invite the Holy Mother to their homes to conduct worship and devotional singing. Coming to know that the Mother would be visiting a certain house, the miscreants would also gather there. One fine evening the Mother visited a house situated in the village Panmana which is about twenty kilometres from Parayakadavu. For a long time the family members of this house had been suffering various physical and mental ailments for which they had been unable to find a solution. They had conducted various pujas to invoke the help of different Gods and Goddesses but to no avail. Coming to hear of the Holy Mother, they had attended the Bhava Darshan and appealed to her for help. The compassionate Mother agreed to come to their house and perform a special puja to eliminate their ailments.

As it turned out, some of the family members were against the worship and joined up with the miscreants who were making preparations to disrupt the worship. On the evening of the Mother's visit one among the family members, full of arrogance, told the Holy Mother, "See, let me observe the worship. I will keenly watch everything. Then I have certain questions to ask." Then the Mother asked him, "Is this 'I' something that is limited only to your body? Is it under your possession?"

It was now two o'clock in the morning and the Mother was preparing all the items for the puja. The person who had made the egotistic declaration fell back in an unconscious state as if in a deep sleep much to the relief of the devoted members of the family. Just as the last step of the puja was completed the arrogant fellow woke up with a start. He jumped up and exclaimed, "Oh, is the worship over? Oh, is it over...?"

The Mother replied, "Yes, it is finished. You said you would watch it keenly. Have you seen it? Now do you understand that the thing we call 'I' is not under our control? When you were sleeping, where did your 'I' go?" The man turned pale and hung his head down without uttering a word.

The miscreants who had also gathered there were not to be put off so easily. They began questioning the Holy Mother in the most rude and irrational manner. The Mother remained ever cheerful and unperturbed but the brahmacharin[44] who had come to assist in the puja became fed up. He requested the Mother, "Please show them something to keep their mouths shut. Otherwise they won't cease their disturbance."

A few more minutes had passed when suddenly there rose up from the nearby graveyard a tremendously blazing fireball. Rays of fire emerged from it as if dancing around the fiery orb. Now it was the Mother's turn to ask a question to the dumbfounded troublemakers. "Those who are courageous among you, why not walk to the graveyard and back?" Not one among them stepped forward to accept the challenge. After a moment, the frightened men-turned-boys stepped back and fled from the place.

Another similar incident occurred in 1980 in the home of Srimati Indira of Karunagapally, a town some ten kilometres from Vallickavu[45]. Indira was an ardent devotee and had invited the Holy Mother to visit her home to bestow sanctity there. As usual, the rationalists also arrived on the appointed evening. The family members became frightened seeing them as their ill reputation was well known. They prayed to the Mother to disperse the band of nonbelievers.

The Mother became absorbed in meditation. Within a couple of seconds to everyone's surprise there appeared a brilliantly shining orb surrounded by many bright lights which looked like tiny lamps. This orb appeared at the northern side of the house

---

[44] Vallickavu is the village on the mainland just opposite Idamannel. The Holy Mother is sometimes called 'Vallickavu Amma'.
[45] A spiritual aspirant who observes the vow of celibacy.

and began moving in a southward direction passing through the front door. The devotees were filled with awe and reverence and uttered the Divine Mother's Name. Slowly the orb flew higher and higher and finally disappeared into the distance but only after it had circumambulated the sacred bilva tree (aegle marmelos) growing in the southern yard. Astounded and frightened, the nonbelievers quit the house. They never returned to disturb the devotional singing of the Mother and in fact, after this incident, many among them also became devotees.

Black Magic Fails

There was a very egotistical sorcerer who lived nearby the previously mentioned house. Somebody had told him of a young girl in Parayakadavu who was possessed by Krishna and Devi three nights a week. The black magician boasted that he would bring a quick end to the possession. He even described the incantation that he would use. "I will split the mid rib of a coconut leaf blade in two while uttering certain powerful mantras and the visit of the God and the Goddess in her body will immediately stop," he declared. Thus he came to Idamannel one day. Try as he might, none of his trickery produced the boasted result and he had to leave after tasting a dose of his own ego. Still he persisted in his witchcraft against the Mother. On several occasions he sent her ash which had been imbued with evil mantras, but all of his attempts failed. Shortly thereafter he himself went crazy and became a beggar in the streets. He would always be heard asking people, "Give me ten paise, give me ten paise..."

There was a priest who lived in Arickal, a village on the same island where the Holy Mother lived. Besides being a temple priest, he was a well known sorcerer who was particularly efficient in driving out evil spirits and subtle beings that had possessed innocent people. It seems that one elderly woman who had a strong disliking for the Holy Mother, secretly approached this priest. Her intention was to persuade him to use his powers to bring the downfall of the Holy Mother and the Divine Bhavas. In order to initiate the conjuration the woman wrote the Holy Mother's Name and birth star on a piece of paper and gave it to the priest.

That same day, one woman devotee of the Mother had a dream wherein the Holy Mother appeared and said that she should go to a particular temple the next day and offer her prayers there. The next day, the devotee came to the Holy Mother and told her about the dream. The Mother told, "You go there and come back. Then you will understand the significance of the dream."

Thus, having taken the permission of the Holy Mother, the woman proceeded to the temple which had been indicated in her dream. Unknown to the devotee, this was the same temple where the priest who had been persuaded to carry out black magic against the Mother conducted the daily worship. Having offered her prayers in the temple, the devotee went to meet the priest in order to discuss a few things. Seeing the devotee, the priest expressed his hospitality and got up from the cot on which he was sitting. He began rolling up the mattress saying "Come, please sit down... please be seated..." As he was rolling up the mattress, a small scrap of paper fell on the ground in front of the devotee. Picking it up, she saw the Holy Mother's name and birth star written on the scrap of paper. Immediately, she understood the import of the paper and the priest-sorcerer and the dream. She began beating her chest saying, "What have you done? Have you done something to our Mother? If so, then we cannot live anymore!" Saying thus she burst into tears. The priest explained, "No, no, I have not done anything. One old lady came here yesterday continuously telling me that I should destroy that place.

In order to get her to quit bothering me, I took this note from her and kept it here."

Calming down on observing the priest's sincerity, she requested him, "Please, you come and see for yourself what is happening there. Then you will understand the truth of the matter." The priest agreed and said he would come there soon and observe the situation directly.

As promised, the priest arrived at Idamannel during one Bhava Darshan. Hearing about the infamous priest's arrival, a big crowd of believers and nonbelievers gathered and anxiously awaited to see the sorcerer's meeting with the Mother. Some people said, "This priest is a great magician. He will put an end to everything that is going on here." The devotees with strong conviction said, "He is not going to do anything."

The priest had come with one elderly woman and he gave her a packet of beaten rice[46] to hold while he entered the temple. The priest had already decided that he would become a devotee of the Mother if she could prove to him that she was really a Divine Being. The Mother was in Krishna Bhava. She gave him a handful of sacred ash and asked, "Are you not here to chant this mantra?" Having said this, she uttered an obscure mantra which was known only to the priest. The priest was taken aback. The Mother continued, "Are you not a worshipper of Hanuman? Do not chant evil mantras with the same tongue which you use to chant His Name." The priest stood there speechless. Nobody in the whole world knew that his Upasana Murthi (Beloved Deity) was Hanuman. The Mother had just revealed the greatest secret in his life. But the Mother was not finished with him. "Have you not asked a lady to stand outside and hold a packet of beaten

---

[46] Grains of rice beaten into flakes resembling rolled oats.

rice? Kuchela[47] went to Sri Krishna with an offering of beaten rice. Have you not come with the same offering of rice? But one thing. Kuchela offered the beaten rice of renunciation and truth to Krishna. Even though the rice was full of stones and sand, the Lord couldn't see it. He looked and could only see Kuchela's pure devotion and open heart. There were neither stones nor sand there. Everything was ambrosia. That is why the Lord ate it. Why did you borrow raw rice from your neighbour? After husking the paddy, why did you mix it with stones and sand and bring it here?"

The priest was incredulous. Hearing all that he had done coming from the mouth of the Holy Mother in exacting detail, he burst into tears. With deep remorse, he sought forgiveness for his evil actions. From that day onwards, he became a true devotee of the Holy Mother.

Further Exploits of the Committee to Stop Blind Beliefs

The Committee to Stop Blind Beliefs now launched more crooked plans against the Holy Mother. They tried to influence high police officials and government authorities to make a move against the Bhava Darshan. The Committee's activity led to several investigations, both public and undercover, but the only outcome to be seen was that many of the investigators became devotees!

One evening as the Devi Bhava was in progress, the trouble-makers demanded that the girl who was singing devotional songs stop. The girl retorted, "I will sing. I have faith in the Holy Mother." A wordy duel started from this incident which

---

[47] An ardent devotee of Lord Krishna whose story appears in the Srimad Bhagavatam.

culminated in a quarrel between the devotees and the rowdies. Finally, Sugunanandan arrived on the scene and chased them away.

Soon after they left, the Holy Mother called her father and warned him, "They have gone to lodge a petition against us. I will be the first defendant and you will be the second. You must go beforehand and inform the authorities of the true situation." Without caring for the words of the Mother, he said, "They won't lodge a case against us. The police won't come here." The Mother insisted several more times and at last, Sugunanandan went to the police station. He found that the Holy Mother's prediction was perfectly true and he presented his case clearly and sincerely.

"We are not cheating anybody. It is true that my daughter is manifesting Divine Moods. Only if you come there yourself will you really understand the truth of the matter. The devotees come and sing devotional songs. There is nothing artificial there. Water taken from the public tap and ash purchased from Oachira are the substances distributed as prasadam[48]. We never materialize flowers from the sky. We offer flowers plucked from the trees and bushes. No advertisement or publicity is given about the Divine Moods. People come after hearing about the experiences of others who have already witnessed the Bhava Darshan. Above all, this takes place in my house. It is nobody else's property. The miscreants come to my house to fight and quarrel with me. Is this justice? Therefore, I request you to protect us from them!"

The officers could not utter a word after hearing what Sugunanandan said and seeing his emphatic sincerity. The false petition was cancelled. The miscreants were furious. In retaliation they launched their next plot to harm the Mother. In those days during the Bhava Darshan after the Holy Mother revealed her oneness with Devi, she would come out from the temple and dance in bliss. One evening, the miscreants came to Idamannel

---

[48] Consecrated offerings blessed by God.

with a basket full of poisonous thorns. These thorns were so sharp and poisonous that even if one pierced a person's foot, he would fall down unconscious.

The thorns were entrusted to a group of local children who had been instructed to scatter them on the ground where the Mother always danced. This was to be done during the Deepa-radhana[49] so that all the attention would be on the Holy Mother and not on the children spreading the thorns. This is exactly what the children did. When the Mother emerged from the temple she gave an intimation to the devotees about what had occurred and admonished them not to move from the place where they stood. With that, the Mother began her ecstatic dance while holding the sword and the trident in her uplifted hands. The dance of the Mother was an awe-inspiring sight. The devotees felt as if Mother Kali Herself, the Destroyer of evil, was dancing before them. She was dancing along the verandah at the front of the temple when suddenly her sword severed the strings which held the pictures on the wall. They came to the ground with a crash scattering broken glass all over the verandah. Unmindful of the hazard, the Mother continued dancing, all the while trampling the broken pieces of glass as if they were merely flower petals.

Those who had come to endanger the Holy Mother were wonderstruck at this sight but still waited full of hope to see her feet bleeding full of thorns and to witness the Mother collapsing on the ground unable to bear the excruciating pain.

Now the Mother stepped down from the temple verandah and came right to the place where the thorns had been scattered. She drew a line on the ground with the tip of her sword and forbade anyone to cross over it. With that, she stepped over the line and danced for a long time trampling the poisonous thorns.

---

[49] The waving of burning camphor before the Holy Mother seated in the temple as Devi.

The miscreants could not believe their eyes. Now they became extremely nervous seeing this blood stirring sight and immediately left the place.

When Sugunanandan realised what was happening, he began running here and there full of dread thinking of his daughter's wounded feet. He came with medicine to treat the wounds, but much to his astonishment he could not find even a trace of a scratch or a prick.

Although the so-called rationalists witnessed many such miracles with their own eyes, they were not ready to relinquish their envy and enmity towards the Mother. From the standpoint of the villagers and the devotees, the extraordinary happenings all around the Mother were a source of wonderment. But for the Mother, ever abiding in the Supreme Reality, these events were all child's play. When some of the devotees came to her full of depression due the endless stream of harassment imposed on their beloved Mother by the unrighteous miscreants, she told, "Children, there is no world without two. We should not be bothered by all these things. Mother's devotees are all around the world. They will not be deluded by all these actions."

The Holy Mother advised the devotees and family members to be calm and patient. They implicitly followed the Mother's advice and silently endured the dreadful conduct of the rationalists.

On another occasion, some of the younger members of the rationalist movement came to Idamannel with a mischievous intention. They had decided to imitate the dance of the Holy Mother during the Bhava thinking that they could deceive the devotees and make a mockery of the Mother.

By the time they arrived, the Darshan had already begun. The Mother was lovingly receiving the devotees one by one. At the same time, she called a few of the devotees and told them of the youths' intention to dance in imitation of her. She forbade the devotees from harming them and sent the devotees outside having given the necessary instructions. These devotees waited with alertness. After some time, one of the youths started to make a show. He tried to imitate certain gestures which the Holy Mother manifested during the Divine Mood. The vigilant devotees surrounded the trickster and began questioning him. Unable to answer their questions, he be came frightened and understood the seriousness of what he had done. All his friends immediately fled the place leaving this boy behind. Running in confusion, he finally jumped into the backwaters! The devotees dragged him out of the water. They gave him a stern warning not to repeat his foolish actions and sent him on his way.

At this time, the miscreants launched their most bold and macabre plan of all. They hired an assassin to enter the temple and stab the Mother to death during the Bhava Darshan. Concealing a knife under his clothes, he entered the temple. Seeing him, the Mother beamed a benign smile at him and continued receiving the devotees. Her smile had a strangely soothing effect on him. Coming to his senses and realizing his grave mistake, he fell at the Mother's feet and begged her forgiveness. When he left the temple, he was a changed man. Noticing the startling change which had come over him, his villainous comrades asked him whether he too had been mesmerized by the Holy Mother. He merely smiled at them and thenceforth became an ardent devotee of the Mother.

During this period, it became impossible for the Holy Mother to walk along the road or village path without being verbally abused by the uncouth troublemakers. They would stand on either side of the road and mock her in a very coarse manner. They even encouraged the young village children to do the same. If it was early morning, they would hide behind trees and bushes and even throw stones at her. This uncultured lot would not limit their torments to the Holy Mother. The whole family fell a prey to their deplorable pastime. Seeing a family member, the miscreants would call out, "Here comes Krishna! Here comes Krishna!"

If the rationalists had no other plan for the evening, they would then enter the temple and make false claims to the Mother hoping to expose her as a fraud. One man came to the Mother and told her that he was blind. The Mother immediately shot out her forefinger as if to poke out his eye. The man jumped back and cried out, "Oh!" Thus, the Mother exposed the fraud of the one who came to defraud her.

On another occasion, a young man came to the Mother and said that he had severe pain in his arm. He expected the Mother to massage his arm believing his words. Instead, she asked a brahmacharin who was standing nearby to rub the man's arm. As soon as the brahmacharin touched his arm, the man experienced severe pain in the exact place that he had described to the Mother. Unable to bear the racking pain, he sought her forgiveness for his childish prank. Without fail, those who came to defraud the Mother were themselves exposed as frauds.

"Today's Enemy Is Tomorrow's Friend"

Sugunanandan became fed up hearing and seeing this perpetual nonsense and evil action of the rationalists. Frustrated, one night during Devi Bhava he approached the Mother and said, "Is this the fruit which God has given me? People call me the murderer of my own son! I cannot walk through the village without constant reproach. This is a pitiful situation. Devi should punish the evildoers!"

The Mother replied, "Wait and see. Today's enemy is tomorrow's friend. Then who should I punish? Those who oppose you today will come and marry your daughters tomorrow. Console yourself thinking that everything happens according to God's Will. If your one son is gone, thousands of sons will come tomorrow." Damayanti was steeped in sorrow over the death of her son. The Holy Mother told her, "Don't be sad. In future, so many children will come here from all over the world. Love them as your own children."

Though the Holy Mother's days and nights were dedicated to bestowing solace and succour upon the devotees, she still found time to serve and extend help to her family members who were facing a critical moment in life. From a worldly point of view, she was a young maiden, yet she did perfect justice to thousands of her devotees and to her own parents as well without even slightly deviating from the path of Truth and righteousness. Her attitude towards her family and the way she looked after them was a source of inspiration for the house holder devotees. The Mother was a spotless example of how one could be spiritual and still fulfil one's duty to one's family while remaining detached and pure.

Though Sugunanandan had a fish marketing business, it was not very profitable. He finally closed it when the Bhava Darshan began bringing large numbers of people from all over the country to his house. Also, he could not concentrate on his business due to the opposition of the villagers and other problems which had cropped up in connection with the Bhava Darshan. He was forced to spend all his time at Idamannel. Besides all this, he still had three daughters yet to be married, though he seemed rather unconcerned. His sons were all in school. Now and then some one of the family would be afflicted with an illness requiring medical attention.

At this juncture, perhaps triggered by all this stress and strain, Sugunanandan was hospitalized in the beginning of 1979 and subsequently had to undergo surgery. The hospital was in Kollam, a city thirty five kilometres south of Vallickavu. There was nobody to help in the household chores or to tend Sugunanandan in the hospital. All the relatives were dead against the family. Kasturi was working in a distant place. Damayanti was bedridden with rheumatic pain. The boys were either too young or studying in school. All the burden fell on the Holy Mother's shoulders.

On Darshan days the devotees began arriving from 1 o'clock onwards. By four in the afternoon the Mother would sit for the devotional singing followed by the Bhava Darshan which would sometimes go on until eight or nine the next morning. Until everybody had been received, the Mother would not stir from her seat in the temple. In between all this, she would give instruction to the spiritual aspirants who came seeking her guidance. After the completion of the Darshan, the Mother would attend to all the household chores just as she had done for so many years. She would get all the younger ones ready and send them off to school. Once all the work had been accomplished, the Mother would go to Kollam bringing food and necessities to Sugunanandan in the hospital. She looked after him with utmost care and sincerely served him throughout his illness.

The miscreants were not ones to miss their chance. When the Mother walked through the village on her way to Kollam, they would mock her and throw stones. They would call out, "Krishna, Krishna..." Silently enduring all their misguided behaviour, the Mother thought, 'At least in this way they are chanting the Lord's Name.' Once, a rowdy even tried to seize the Holy Mother, but when he jumped forward to catch her, he slipped and fell into the roadside ditch.

Gradually, Sugunanandan regained his health. However, shortly thereafter Damayanti was also hospitalized followed by Suresh. Throughout this period, it was the Mother who looked after all household duties and served the hospitalized family members.

Chaos and confusion prevailed in the family atmosphere but no matter what the situation, the Mother remained a solid pillar of support and sustenance, ever calm and compassionate. Imagine the situation. The uproar created by Subhagan's suicide, the non cooperation of the relatives, the antagonism of the rationalists, the flocking of thousands of devotees for the Bhava Darshan, and three unmarried daughters in the house. It is no wonder that nobody was eager to make a marriage alliance with this family! If somebody came with a marriage proposal from a distant place, by the time they reached Idamannel, certain members of the village had met up with them to discourage them from their proposal. Several prospective grooms had beat a quick retreat.

And so it was that Sugunanandan again approached the Holy Mother and said, "Because of the Bhava Darshan, I have lost my honour. I cannot even show my face outside of Idamannel. The villagers as well as the relatives hate me and my daughters remain unmarried. What am I to do?"

The Holy Mother replied, "It is not the Bhava Darshan which is the cause of all your misfortune. Everything moves according to Divine Will. All will take place at the proper time. You do not have to worry." Sugunanandan was not to be consoled this time. He angrily shouted, "I will drink poison and die!" Hearing this, the Mother turned to a portrait of Devi and asked with tear-filled eyes, "O Compassionate Mother, am I bringing only sorrow to these people?"

Occasions were not rare when the Mother decided to leave Idamannel and even began making preparations to do so. But each time, this act was mysteriously blocked. Again Sugunanandan approached the Mother with his anxiety. Again she told,

"Do not worry. The marriage of your daughters will take place without much delay."

Within a month, the words of the Mother came true. A marriage proposal came for Sugunamma from the most unexpected family. This family was dead against the Holy Mother and the bridegroom was one of the ringleaders of the rationalist movement. Ironically, now that the marriage was fixed, Sugunanandan dropped out of the picture. The complete responsibility for arranging the actual wedding fell to the Holy Mother! Established as she was in a state of perfect equanimity, it seemed that there was nothing which could shake the initiative and efficiency of the Mother. The marriage ceremony went off successfully despite the fact that Sugunanandan stood on the side lines casually observing the whole event.

The Holy Mother's words, "Today's enemy is tomorrow's friend," came true and the same was repeated for the other daughters' marriages as well.

There is a saying in Malayalam, 'The jasmine which grows in the front of the house has no fragrance.' The meaning of this is that if a person becomes great and famous, he will never be recognized by his or her own community. Many are the righteous souls who have suffered the truth of the adage. The Holy Mother would say, "Suppose somebody was listening to a beautiful song on the radio. He was really enjoying the sweetness of the song's melody when his close friend came into the room and said, 'Do you know who is singing that song? It is our neighbour, Shankar.' Immediately, the one who was enjoying the song turned off the radio saying, 'Oh, what kind of a singer is he? It's terrible!' Children, this is the attitude of the people. It is difficult for them to accept a person who they have always known and moved closely with." Thus it was in the case of the Holy Mother.

The circumstances that surrounded the Mother were far from kind. This young fisherfolk girl was supported by none. As

170

the devotees were from different parts of the country, they could do nothing against the ignorant and uncultured villagers who tormented the Holy Mother. Besides that, the devotees for the most part believed that the Mother was possessed by Krishna and Devi during the Bhava Darshan. They failed to understand the depth or fullness of the Mother's God Realisation. Not only that; most of the devotees in those early days came primarily for worldly achievements, not spiritual upliftment. If their desire was fulfilled, they would return only when another desire cropped up. If their desire didn't get fulfilled, then they would never come again and their devotion to the Mother ended there. The Mother had neither an inch of her own land nor a penny at her disposal. Her own kith and kin were non cooperative and deadly opposed her. Her own family members were against her wish and will. They neither helped nor encouraged her in any way.

On one occasion, a devotee asked the Mother about the immensity of the trials and tribulations which she had to confront both during and after her sadhana days. They wondered how their own Realisation could ever take place if they had to undergo so much suffering which they doubted they could forbear. Mother was quick to point out that her own life only showed that it was possible to realize God even under the worst possible circumstances.

It will be of great interest to the readers to know how the Holy Mother raised an ashram from the midst of this raging storm and this will be related in the next chapter.

Chapter Ten

The Mother of
Immortal Bliss

*"Always understand that Mother is omnipresent.
Have the faith that Mother's Self and your Self
are one. Children, the mother who gave birth to
you may look after matters relating to this life;
nowadays even this is very rare. But Mother's aim
is to lead you in such a way that you can enjoy
bliss in all your future lives."*

– Mata Amritanandamayi

Trailōkya sphuta vaktāro
devādyasura pannagāha
guruvaktra sthitā vidyā
gurubhaktyā tu labhyatye

The Guru's Wisdom cannot be learned
From even gods of the higher worlds;
The Guru's Knowledge awakes in him
Who serves his Guru with purest love.

— Guru Gita, verse 22

A Band Of Youths

"Children, the coolness of the breeze, the beams of the
moon, the vastness of space and all things of the world—
these are all permeated with Divine Consciousness.
Knowing and experiencing this Truth is the Goal
of human birth. In this dark age a band of youths,
renouncing all, will set out to disseminate spiritual light
throughout the world."

— Mata Amritanandamayi

As early as 1976, a young boy of twenty named Unni Krishnan from the village of Alappad came to meet the Holy Mother. He was rather like a mendicant. Although he had a home and family, he only rarely visited them. After meeting the Holy Mother, he developed a strong thirst to lead a spiritual life. The Holy Mother understood this and entrusted him, a year later, with the daily worship in the temple, allowing him to remain in her presence at Idamannel. He spent his days inside the small shrine performing the daily worship and reciting the Sri Lalita Sahasranamam[50], as the Holy Mother had instructed him. He did other spiritual practices as well, read scriptural texts, and wrote devotional poetry. At night, he slept on the temple verandah using only a thin towel spread on the floor as a mattress. He was so calm and quiet that none of the visitors knew he was staying there. In this way, he became the first resident of the future ashram. By the end of 1978, the nucleus of the ashram grew when a group of well-educated young men, renouncing home and life in the world, took refuge at the feet of the Holy Mother with God-Realisation and service to humanity their one aim. Attracted by the magnetic personality and all-embracing love of the Holy Mother, these young men were inspired to lead a divine life against great odds. Most of them were from the town of Haripad[51], and came from upper class families. After meeting the Holy Mother, they knew with strong conviction that the path shown by the Mother was the ultimate goal that they could aspire to in their lives.

Within one month Sreekumar, Ramesh Rao, Venugopal, Ramakrishnan and Balagopalan (Balu)[52] came to meet the Holy Mother and humbly requested her to guide them to their chosen goal. However, Sugunanandan discouraged them from staying permanently near the Holy Mother. His reluctance was motivated by the fact that his other daughters were not yet married. These young aspirants were either still in college or holding jobs, except

[50] Sacred mantra consisting of the thousand Names of the Divine Mother.
[51] Situated 20 kilometers north of Vallickavu.
[52] Now known as Swami Amritasvarupananda Puri after receiving a traditional initiation into sannyasa from the Holy Mother.

for Balu, who had just completed his college studies. They would come to see the Mother nearly every day or every other day while at the same time continuing to fulfil their responsibilities in the world.

For the most part, their sudden transformation from worldly youth to seekers of God created havoc among their family and friends. In their minds, the Holy Mother was a witch who had hypnotized their sons through the use of her master sorcery. Ever ready to find fault with the Holy Mother, the rationalists took up the cause. They began feeding the news media sensational stories in order to provoke public reaction against the Holy Mother.

The devotees and young men became worried about the appearance of these fabricated stories in the newspaper. When the Mother came to know of their anxiety, she burst into laughter and said, "We are not those letters and words printed on a piece of paper. Continue your spiritual practices without wasting your time paying attention to such things. Those who oppose today will become devotees tomorrow." As the days passed, this declaration of the Holy Mother became perfectly true.

In November of that year, a college student came to Idamannel to meet the Holy Mother. The first visit itself created a great transformation in him. He came to visit the Mother now and then whenever possible. He developed an intense desire to relinquish worldly life and sought the advice of the Holy Mother as to where he could stay in order to do his spiritual practices as, in those days, it was Sugunanandan's habit to chase away any young aspirant who desired to stay in the presence of the Holy Mother. He also had to face Sugunanandan's scolding one evening and had been ordered to leave Idamannel. Greatly pained at heart, he asked the Holy Mother to suggest a suitable place for him to continue his practice. She directed him to Tiruvannamalai, the abode of the great Sage Ramana Maharshi, and instructed him to observe a vow of silence for forty-one days.

Before leaving, he asked, "Mother, if Sugunanandan continues to act like this towards the devotees, how will this place ever become an ashram? He is unkind to you and to those who want to stay near you. Mother, how many hardships you are undergoing nowadays! I can't bear to see your sufferings. Is there no one to take care of you and look after your needs?"

The Mother consoled him saying, "Do not worry. Everything will become all right after you return from Tiruvannamalai. In that place there are people who will look after Mother and the future ashram. My children from other countries are there anxiously waiting to see me. The day will come when Sugunanandan will welcome you with all love and affection.

He then requested the Mother for a watch so that he could keep up his daily routine and for a rosary of rudraksha beads[53] for repeating his mantra. The Holy Mother said, "Do not ask Mother for such things or even think of them. A good aspirant will never move from his seat. Whatever he needs is bound to come. Look at the spider and the python. They never go out in search of prey. The spider quietly sits in its web and the small insects come and get trapped in it. It is the duty of God to take care of His devotees. Dedicate everything at His Feet, go to Arunachala and everything necessary will come to you."

Cherishing the Mother's image in his heart and remembering her boundless love, the young man left for Tiruvannamalai using the money given to him by a friend for that purpose. Reaching the sacred abode of Lord Siva, he spent a few days in a cave on the sacred mountain Arunachala. The first two days he subsisted only on leaves and water. On the third day, in the evening, for lack of

---

[53] A dark brown seed which is known for its beneficial effects, both physical and spiritual.

food he fainted calling aloud, 'Amma!' In a letter to the Mother he wrote, "It was about five o'clock in the afternoon when I fainted due to hunger. I was lying on the mountain in a semiconscious state. Just then, I clearly heard Mother's voice calling, 'My son!' I felt that my forehead was being gently rubbed by someone. When I opened my eyes I saw Mother standing before me in her white clothes. I was extremely thrilled at the sight!"

After the Holy Mother received this letter, the devotees understood that it was exactly at that moment in Vallickavu when the Holy Mother had suddenly called out, "Oh my son!" and turned to a devotee sitting nearby saying, "My son is in Tiruvannamalai and has been starving since three days and now he is crying to see me!" After this incident, he never had any difficulty to get food regularly.

In the absence of a proper place to do his spiritual practices, the youth would spend his days on the mountain and his nights sleeping at the foot of the hill. Coming down from the mountain, the first person that he met was an Australian woman named Gayatri. After a couple of days he met Madhusudhana[54], a native of Reunion Island, whose descendants had come from India. All three felt a stream of love binding them together. Recalling the words of the Holy Mother, he had a strong feeling that both of them were her children. He began talking to them about the Holy Mother and showed them a small photo of her. Gayatri was enchanted by the blissful countenance and the glowing eyes of the Mother in the photo.

Although Gayatri would regularly try to meditate, she was not satisfied with her spiritual progress. After seeing the Holy Mother's photo and hearing about her selfless love and compassion, Gayatri had her first spiritual experience. To put it in her own words, "I saw a flash of light within me and discerned the

---

[54] Now known as Prematma Chaitanya.

living form of the Mother in that light. Suddenly from within me arose the cry, 'Amma! Amma! Amma!' Then all thoughts subsided and my mind sank into stillness. When I opened my eyes and looked at the clock, I realised that twenty minutes had passed. I had been unaware of anything."

Madhu, eager to share the happiness which he experienced while hearing about the Holy Mother, introduced the young man to an American devotee named Nealu who was contemplative by nature. His spiritual teacher, who was a direct disciple of Sri Ramana Maharshi, had passed away four years earlier. Serving his teacher, Nealu had been living in Tiruvannamalai for the past eleven years. At this time, he was mostly bedridden suffering from acute pain in the stomach and spine. He was hardly able to sit or walk even for a few moments. The doctors were at a loss to know the cause or cure.

Coming to know of his difficulty to find a place for meditation, Nealu offered his late teacher's cottage for his use. The boy told him about the Holy Mother but Nealu was at first not very interested. He had already seen many great saints and was only concerned to cure his illness so that he could continue with his sadhana. With that idea in mind, he asked him to take him to meet the Holy Mother after the completion of the young man's vow of silence. Then Nealu gave the young sadhak (aspirant) a clock and rudraksha mala thinking that these items may be helpful in his spiritual practice. Recalling the Holy Mother's words that all would come unasked, the boy felt overwhelmed with emotion and earnestly started his vow.

One day while circumambulating Arunachala, he noticed a tall white man chanting Tamil verses while moving with a group of people around the hill. It was the day of Sri Ramana's birthday celebrations. When he glanced at the man, he also looked back at him, though with an air of pride. The young sadhak thought,

"Though proud, he too seems to be the son of the Holy Mother." This man was, in fact, a devotee from France named Ganga who later came to stay near the Holy Mother.

After forty-one days of silence had been observed, the young devotee of the Mother and Nealu journeyed to Vallickavu. Nealu's first meeting with the Holy Mother was highly significant[55]. As he himself describes, "The first four days I spent there, I felt as if I was in Heaven itself, such was the bliss experienced in the Mother's Presence! One evening at the end of Devi Bhava, Mother was standing at the door of the temple and I was standing outside gazing at her with joined palms. I was overflowing with joy. At that moment, I saw her physical form disappear into an expanding radiance which spread all around and engulfed everything visible. That expansive light suddenly contracted into a blazing pinpoint of unbearably dazzling light and then I felt as if that light had entered into me. For three days I could get no sleep due to the spiritual intoxication of that experience. After this, I could think only of the Holy Mother day and night. I decided to be near her until the end of my life in order to take guidance from her and serve her."

Nealu returned to Tiruvannamalai with the boy to settle his affairs and came back to Vallickavu accompanied by Gayatri who was keenly desirous of serving the Holy Mother. Strangely enough, Sugunanandan welcomed all of them as if they were his own children. For the first time in three years, Nealu felt some relief from his sickness and could move about doing small works.

When Nealu returned from Tiruvannamalai, he expressed his wish to the Holy Mother, "I do not want to go away from here. I want to stay with you forever as your humble servant."

---

[55] A detailed description can be found in the book, "On the Road to Freedom" by Swami Paramatmananda, M.A. Mission Trust, India

The Mother told him, "Son, I don't have an inch of land that is my own. Ask the father. Anyhow, we need a place to stay."

It was a great surprise to everyone when Sugunanandan agreed to donate a small piece of land on which was built a modest hut of woven coconut palm leaves. All told, it measured nine by eighteen feet. One corner was used as a kitchen for preparing drinks for the Holy Mother, but daily meals were still prepared in the main house. This hut served as shelter for the Holy Mother along with Nealu, Balu and Gayatri. This marked the informal beginning of the ashram.

After his first meeting with the Holy Mother, Balu left his home and spent most of his time with the Mother. It was his good fortune to get the permission of Sugunanandan to remain at Idamannel on a permanent basis. Thus, when Nealu came from Tiruvannamalai to stay permanently, Balu also settled there.

After the arrival of Nealu and Gayatri, Ganga and Madhu also came and settled at the feet of the Holy Mother. Even though they offered their wealth to the Holy Mother with all devotion, she declined to accept it saying, "If you attain a pure character and become perfect spiritually, that will be my wealth. If one realizes the Essence within himself, he will see It in all. The whole world will become his own."

One night, a man from a neighboring house woke up Ganga in order to borrow his torch (flashlight). The man's daughter was suffering from an acute asthma attack and had to be rushed off to the hospital in the dark. After a few hours, the man came back and returned the torch. The next morning Ganga told Mother about the incident and added that he had felt like breaking the man's head for disturbing his sleep. The Mother scolded him saying,

"What kind of spiritual aspirant are you? What have you gained by leading a spiritual life for so many years before coming here? Is this the fruit of that? Being a follower of the Path of Knowledge as you seem to think you are, you should see everything as your own Self. If this is so, how could you be angry with that man? If your foot was pricked by a sharp thorn, would you not feel the pain and be restless to remove it? Imagine that man's anxiety to relieve his daughter of her suffering. The pain and suffering of all living beings should be felt to be your own. Only then will your mind expand and become as the sky which accommodates all equally. For that, your mind should become innocent like a child's and this is possible only through pure devotion to God."

Ganga replied in a mocking tone, "Devotion is not at all intellectually satisfying. To follow the Path of Devotion shows a certain weakness. Why all these emotional expressions like weeping and singing? I cannot do that. Sri Ramana never prescribed the Path of Devotion. He would only prescribe the Path of Knowledge to his devotees. I prefer the Path of Knowledge as it appeals to the intellect. It is more convincing." Such was Ganga's misconception of devotion at the time of his coming to the Mother.

Mother smilingly retorted,

"I have just seen the fruit of your practice of the Path of Knowledge. If this is the result, then you need not bother about leading a life of sacrifice and renunciation. You may as well enjoy all the pleasures of the senses! Did you read all the writings by and about Sri Ramana? If not, then please do so, for there are many works which are full of devotion. In fact, he himself was an embodiment of devotion to Lord Arunachala. Even the mere mention of that Name would bring tears of Divine Love to his eyes. Devotion is not an indication of mental weakness as you seem to think. It is the greatest achievement that a human can attain. It is perceiving God in all beings equally; it is pure love of Selfless Existence. Son, you should cultivate love within yourself."

Sri Mata Amritanandamayi – A Biography

Not convinced by the Holy Mother's words, Ganga went to Tiruvannamalai. Much to his surprise, he happened to come across a devotional work of Sri Ramana's. Recollecting the Mother's words, he was filled with an overwhelming feeling of love and began weeping. He prayed to the Mother to call him back to her Holy Presence. It was at this time that the Mother, knowing his mental state, wrote a letter asking Ganga to return. Clearly realizing her greatness, he surrendered himself at her feet with all humility.

Madhu had met many saints before coming to the Holy Mother, but when he saw the Mother for the first time he felt as though he had come to the end of his journey. Dedicating his heart and soul to the Mother, Madhu began to collect all the extant commentaries on the Srimad Bhagavad Gita and to trans- late them into French for the spiritual benefit of French devotees. Inspired by the Holy Mother, he spread her spiritual mission in his native land of Reunion and built a beautiful Ashram there dedicated to her. With the blessings of the Holy Mother, he has been instrumental in bringing many people to the spiritual path.

In those days, the Holy Mother spent most of her nights outdoors. Therefore, everyone preferred to sleep beneath the co- conut palms in the sand. Even if the Mother happened to take rest in the hut, by the middle of the night she would get up and walk outside to lie down on the open ground. It remained a fact that the Holy Mother slept very little, ate very little and gave unstintingly of herself. Even after sitting in the temple receiving the devotees three times a week for the entire night, she always made time during the day to receive the devotees and to instruct the spiritual aspirants who sought her guidance.

In the beginning stages, Nealu and Gayatri had a lot of lan- guage problems. They always sought the help of Balu to converse with the Holy Mother, but before long, they slowly began picking up the Mother's language, Malayalam. During this period, Balu was very lucky to serve the Holy Mother as there was nobody else to look after her needs.

One day, Sugunanandan rudely remarked that he was unwilling to feed the 'saippus' (foreigners). Thereafter, Gayatri began preparing food in the hut for the Holy Mother, Nealu, Balu and herself. The Mother ate almost nothing. Sometimes at the insistence of Nealu or Balu she would eat a little, for name sake only.

One day, Nealu continued insisting that the Mother should eat some food. Finally, the Mother said, "Yes, I will eat. Bring something." Without delay, Nealu brought a plateful of food for the Mother. Strangely enough, she finished everything in the twinkling of an eye. Nealu again served food to the Mother. That also was consumed in no time. The Mother looked expectantly at Nealu without moving from her seat. More food was served. This was also eaten. The Mother ate and ate but whatever was served seemed to leave her unsatisfied! Nealu and the others looked at each other in astonishment. More food was brought from the nearby tea-shop. That also was consumed by the Mother without delay. Nealu was exhausted! He turned pale. Never again did he insist that the Holy Mother eat!

During this period, family conflicts again cropped up. Only two months had passed since the marriage of Sugunamma when Sugunanandan hastily arranged the marriages of his other two daughters. Without anybody's consent, he fixed the marriage of his eldest daughter Kasturi. Even the Holy Mother was informed only after Sugunanandan's acceptance had been conveyed to the bridegroom's party.

The problem was, how to conduct the marriage without any money? Sugunanandan had no income and there was no money in the temple. As was his habit, Sugunanandan stepped out of the picture at this juncture. The Mother was unperturbed. Witnessing this, Balu became very sad and asked, "Mother, what is the plan? How to conduct the marriage?" Nealu told, "Mother, I will give whatever I have. It is the duty of the disciple to look after and discharge the responsibilities of his Guru. I have nothing to call my own; whatever I have is Mother's. Therefore, please perform Kasturi's marriage with the money which I have at my disposal."

The Holy Mother replied, "After the marriage, the girls will lead a worldly life. What you have is the wealth meant for spirituality. That must be spent only for righteous purposes. If it is given to worldly people, they will incur sin. That will affect us and our path as well. If it is God who made the father fix the marriage, let God conduct it. We do not have to pay attention to it. Sugunanandan is not much bothered by it; then why should we worry? Children, we do not have to be perplexed about the matter."

Though Sugunanandan was in a haste to fix the marriage, when it came to the more important details like the finances, one could find him standing on the sidelines. The Mother began organizing the needful without uttering a word. Seeing this, Balu became pained at heart and told the Mother, "I will bring my inheritance from my house." The Holy Mother was in complete disagreement. Then Balu wrote to some close devotees requesting financial assistance. Later, when the Mother came to know of this, she scolded him for this action saying, "Son, let us confront it calmly. There is nothing to be excited about."

At last, everything was ready except one item, five thousand rupees. This amount was absolutely necessary to meet the expenses of the wedding. After a few days passed, a check for five thousand rupees was received from an anonymous donor from Madras who had recently heard about the Holy Mother. Thus, in mid-September of 1980, Kasturi was married.

Not three months had passed when Sugunanandan fixed Sajani's marriage. That done, he repeated his disappearing act and left the difficult part to the Holy Mother. The responsibility for accumulating enough money to give as dowry, to pay the expense of the wedding ceremony and to craft the bride's gold ornaments all fell on the Holy Mother's shoulders.

Balu no longer felt sad, he felt angry! The Mother was also displeased by Sugunanandan's lack of discrimination. Though annoyed, the Mother remained unruffled and discharged the task with efficacy. The bridegroom's party asked for more gold. As usual, money remained a big question mark. The Holy Mother was very particular that not a penny be spent from what had been put aside for righteous purposes. Nor would she allow any money to be borrowed. Then what to do?

At this juncture, Kasturi returned to Idamannel from her husband's place due to some difference of opinion. Coming to know of the need for more gold she told, "See, for the time being you can take my ornaments to conduct Sajani's marriage. It is enough if you return them later." Now, everything except one necklace and one ring was at hand. Two days before the marriage these items were yet to be had; still the Mother was calm and detached as ever. The next morning when the Bhava Darshan was over Gayatri, who was cleaning the temple, noticed a small package lying among the offerings. Opening it, what was her surprise to find a necklace and ring fitting the exact description of what was needed for the marriage! Even the style of the ornaments was the same as had been selected a month ago! What other proof was needed to show that the Divine Will arranges for everything?

However, this was not the end of the difficulties which plagued this final wedding. Some among the local devotees raised an objection with Sugunanandan. Why had he fixed a marriage alliance with those who had previously been enemies? Were the sons of the well-wishers and devotees not good enough for him? Some young men who had been close friends of Subhagan had wished to marry Sugunanandan's daughters. Now they also turned against him. Thus, when enemies became relatives those who were friends became enemies. They came to quarrel with Sugunanandan and conspired to create obstacles for Sajani's marriage. Hoping to annul the marriage, they spread scandalous stories and sent the same to the bridegroom. Even the day before the wedding everyone was full of doubt whether or not the marriage would be performed.

On the day of the marriage, the Holy Mother took the brahmacharis to the neighboring house. For the two previous marriages she had done the same. This was for the benefit of the brahmacharis who should not attend such ceremonies.

The Mother explained,

"An aspirant should not take part in marriage ceremonies or funerals. At the former, everyone will be thinking of the marriage, which is a bondage. At the latter, the grief is about the loss of a mortal being. In both cases, the participants are dwelling on the non-eternal. These thought waves will be harmful to a seeker. The worldly vibrations will enter the subconscious mind. The seeker will become restless for unreal things."

Thus, the main impediment for the brahmacharis to take up permanent residence in the Holy Mother's presence had been removed. All three of Sugunanandan's daughters were now married. Not only that. The miscreants and rationalists, accepting utter failure, retreated one by one. Some among them understood that their irrational actions were meaningless and left the organization forever. The remaining members began fighting among themselves and thus the 'Committee to Stop Blind Beliefs' was totally dissolved. Those who came to fight against Truth and Righteousness became the cause of their own destruction. These developments marked the beginning of a new phase in the Holy Mother's spiritual service to relieve and uplift ailing humanity.

Mother's attitude towards all the trials and tribulations which she suffered from her relatives and miscreants over the years is unique. One day she narrated,

"It was their misguided conceptions that made them speak and behave the way they did and also because they could not realize the significance and purport of spiritual life. Such being the case, why should we be angry with them or dislike them? It would be our ignorance to do so and as a result our minds would only get polluted. Look at these fresh roses. How beautiful they are! What a fine fragrance they exude! But what do we give them to make them grow? Just a little used tea leaves and cow dung! What a vast difference between these beautiful flowers and the manure given to them! Compared to their beauty and fragrance, is this manure befitting them? Likewise, impediments are the fertilizer which makes us grow stronger spiritually. These obstacles will all help our hearts to blossom fully. Chirping at night is the nature of crickets but that sound never disturbs anybody's sleep. Likewise, to create trouble is the nature of the ignorant. We must therefore pray to God to forgive them and to lead them to the right path. Dedicate everything to God and He will look after you."

The Mother of Immortal Bliss

It now became possible for the first group of brahmacharis to settle at the feet of the Holy Mother due to the relative peace of mind that Sugunanandan enjoyed since the marriage of his daughters. Despite the fact that there were no accommodations, due to the brahmacharis' keen interest to be in the company of the Holy Mother, they took no notice of the fact that food, clothing and shelter were minimal. Most of the time, they had to live outdoors and sleep on the bare ground without even a mat. Whatever was received came unasked and was shared amongst themselves. Having no money, if any of them had to go somewhere, they would walk. Even though they had only one set of clothes each, somehow they learned to manage.

Feeling a bit depressed one day that his only set of clothes was dirty and worn, one of the brahmacharis complained to the Mother about the lack of necessities. The Mother replied, "Son, do not ask for such small things from God. Surrender yourself at His Feet and He will give you whatever you really need." The Holy Mother had lived that way herself and therefore spoke only from her own experience. The very next day a devotee brought a new set of clothes for all the brahmacharis although he had been unaware of the situation at the time.

These boys received an all-around training in renunciation due to the austere circumstances in which they lived during the early days of the ashram. In order to give them courage, the Holy Mother told them, "If you can withstand this here, you can be at home anywhere. If you can overcome any adverse situation now, then you will easily cope with any crisis or challenge of life."

As the number of devotees and resident brahmacharis went on increasing and the lack of facilities stayed the same, the idea to formally incorporate as an Ashram was born. However, the situation did not look very promising. The Holy Mother had neither land nor wealth at her disposal. Even the land where Nealu had built the hut belonged to Sugunanandan. Although he had given permission for Nealu, Balu and Gayatri to stay at Idamannel permanently, Sugunanandan had never entertained the idea that his home would become a future ashram. The thought of accommodating more and more people did not hold his fancy either. Once when the Holy Mother was discussing the idea of an ashram, he angrily made his point very clear, "What is this! Do we have any wealth or riches here? How to run an ashram? Where shall we (the family) go if this becomes an ashram? No! I shall not agree to register an ashram here!"

Initially, the Holy Mother was not in favour of the idea to become a formal ashram either. When some amongst the devotees approached her with the proposal, she replied, "Mother has heard a lot about 'ashram'. Mother does not need an ashram. Is it not a bondage? Haven't you seen the palmist walking with the caged parrot, i.e. being bound for another person's purpose? At last, Mother's situation will also become like that. I cannot do that. Mother has her own freedom. There should be no obstacle for that."

However, as the flow of devotees and disciples swelled, it was not long before the need of an organized ashram became an unavoidable necessity. Furthermore, the Holy Mother's foreign disciples, according to the law of the land, were prohibited from staying in a private house for any appreciable length of time. At this point the Holy Mother herself became convinced of the need for a government approved spiritual centre. The Mother's opinion was sought as to how to proceed. She mischievously replied, "Anyhow, the family members will not establish an ashram. Their samskara *(mental make-up)* is different. Let us not wait for their permission; they will never cooperate. But we may have to hear a little of their scolding!"

Thus, on the 6th of May in the year of 1981, with a view to preserving and propagating the ideals and teachings of the Holy Mother, the Mata Amritanandamayi Math and Mission Trust was founded and registered under the Travancore-Cochin State Literary and Charitable Act of 1955, at Kollam, Kerala, South India. From this time onwards, the Holy Mother officially adopted the name 'Mata Amritanandamayi' which was given to her by one of her brahmacharin sons. Already being the Mother of Immortal Bliss, as her name denotes, the name was indeed befitting.

Around this time, one of the brahmacharins, being in need of some scriptural books, requested Mother to select a number for him from a lottery in which the winner would be presented with some books. Mother told him, "Why crave for such things? You will soon receive plenty of books." It was shortly after this incident that Nealu, who came to stay permanently with Mother from Tiruvannamalai, decided to shift his library of more than two thousand books in English and various Indian languages from that place to the ashram in Vallickavu. Thus, the Ashram Library came into being.

On the 27th of August, 1982, a Vedanta Vidyalaya (School) was started in order to impart traditional Vedantic and Sanskrit knowledge to the residents of the ashram. All the same, Mother always reminds the brahmacharins of the importance of meditation instead of mere book learning. The ashram routine consists of six to eight hours of meditation for all the residents. Those who would like to devote all of their time for meditation are by all means encouraged and there are a few such in the ashram. Mother says,

"Scriptures are just like signboards. They are only a means but not an end in themselves. The end is something beyond them. A student of agriculture knows how to sow the seeds, when and how to put the fertilizer, how to get rid of pests and prevent their return, etc. Likewise, study of scriptures gives us directions as to how to do our spiritual practices."

A word should be said about the vast change which has come over the Holy Mother's family and the villagers. Realizing her to be divine, they now feel proud of the fact that they are related to her or living in the same village. Sugunanandan and Damayanti often wonder what meritorious acts they performed in their past lives in order to become the 'parents' of the Divine Mother Herself! They are now exemplary householders and lovingly play the role of a father and mother to all of the brahmacharins who stay in the ashram, regarding them as their own children.

Today, Mata Amritanandamayi Math and Mission Trust is a growing spiritual centre headed by the Divine Mother who is very particular to see that it is run according to the ancient traditions of this holy land of India. All the ashram work is attended to by the residents themselves who each put in at least one hour of work each day for the maintenance of the ashram, cooking, cleaning, tending the cows, etc. The ashram is looked upon by Mother's many devotees as their spiritual home and as a fertile field where noble spiritual qualities can be abundantly cultivated, and the fruit of God-Realisation reaped.

Responding to the repeated requests of her children from abroad, the Holy Mother made her first world tour during May-August 1987. She travelled widely in the USA and Europe. The impact was wonderful. The Holy Mother inspired and transformed many people who experienced her unique spiritual charm and universal love on a vast scale. In December 1987, the Holy Mother visited Reunion Island and Mauritius at the request of the Mata Amritanandamayi Mission Center, which has been functioning there since 1985 under the leadership of one of her disciples. Subsequently, the Holy Mother made three more world tours in 1988, 1989 and 1990. A beautiful residential retreat center, the Mata Amritanandamayi Center, has also come into existence about a forty-five minute drive from San Francisco, California.

To those blessed souls who find their way to Mother's Holy Presence, she graciously advises them:

"Beholding a block of stone, a master sculptor will see only the beautiful form latent in it ignoring its rough exterior. Likewise, a God-Realised Soul sees only the ever-shining Atman or

Self in all without distinction, ignoring the external differences. A drunkard cannot propagate prohibition of liquor. He should himself abstain from drinking first and then only can he ask others to do the same. Likewise, my children, only after you yourselves become morally and spiritually perfect and behold Divinity in all, can you teach others to become so."

Let this life story of the Holy Mother be concluded with her loving call to the entire human race:

"Come quickly my darling children, you
who are the Divine Essence of 'OM'.
Removing all sorrows, grow to be adorable
and merge with the sacred 'OM'!"

Chapter Eleven

The Meaning of the Divine Bhavas

The Divine Bhavas of the Holy Mother as Krishna and Devi are a subject beyond the reach of the human intellect, yet a thoughtful study of them gives us a glimpse into the Holy Mother's infinite spiritual power. Responding to the sincere call of the devotee, a Perfect Master slowly reveals His infinite attributes to the heart of the devotee. When the process of purification becomes intense, the Guru's greatness, which is nothing but the True Nature of the disciple or devotee, will gradually be revealed by the Grace of the Master. Grace, of course, is the primary requisite for beginning to grasp the significance of the Holy Mother's Divine Moods.

The Great Masters of India have classified Divine Incarnations in three main categories: 1) Purna Avatara (full or perfect), 2) Amsa Avatara (partial manifestation), and 3) Avesa Avatara (temporary overshadowing by divine power). The word 'Avatara' means coming down or descent. A Purna Avatara is the descent of the nameless, formless and immutable Supreme Energy, assuming a human form and manifesting infinite power without any limitations. The intention of such a One is to restore and preserve righteousness (dharma) and awaken humanity by making people aware of the higher Self. Amsa Avatara is the coming down of God while partially manifesting some of His power in order to fulfil a particular purpose or goal. The Incarnations of Lord Vishnu as Vamana (the Dwarf) and Narasimha (Man-lion) are typical examples of Amsa Avataras. Avesa Avatara is entirely different from these two types of Incarnations. This is the temporary visitation or possession by divine beings, who use the body of some people in order to fulfil certain tasks. Lord Vishnu's Incarnation as Parasurama, as depicted in the epic Srimad Bhagavatam, is a example of this type. Here, the Lord entered the body of Parasurama, who was a great warrior, in order to destroy the cruel kshatriya kings who had become very arrogant and egotistic. Soon after he had fulfilled this task, the power left him. It is said that Sri Rama, another Incarnation of Lord Vishnu, took the divine power back from Parasurama while returning to Ayodhya after his marriage with Sita. The scriptures say that demons or ghosts sometimes possess the body of people who are mentally weak. People who are predominantly virtuous and good in nature (sattvic) will be possessed by devas (minor gods), those endowed with creativity and vigour (rajasic) may be possessed by celestial being (inferior to minor gods), and people whose nature is full of darkness and obscurity (tamasic) may be possessed by evil spirits. The scriptures also mention that in the body of rare souls who are extremely pure, Divine Power may manifest for a short period of time. This is why Parasurama is considered to be an Avesa Avatara.

The following is an illustration which might help the reader to gain insight into the Holy Mother's Divine Bhavas. Once when Lord Krishna was living in Dwaraka, he cherished a desire to see his dear devotee, Hanuman. His vehicle, Garuda, the king of birds, was sent as his messenger to Kadali Vanam, where Hanuman was residing, but Hanuman refused to go. He explained,

"I won't go to see anyone other than my Lord Rama". When the reply of Hanuman was conveyed to Lord Sri Krishna, He once again sent the bird chief to Hanuman saying, "You tell him that Lord Sri Rama with His holy consort Sita have come to Dwaraka and They would like to see Hanuman."

While Garuda was fetching Hanuman, certain events were taking place in Dwaraka. Lord Krishna, by His mere Will, assumed the form of Lord Rama, who had lived many centuries earlier. Rukmini, Krishna's consort, became Sita. By this time, Hanuman had arrived in Dwaraka. Having seen his beloved Sri Rama and Sita and having offered worship to Them, he returned to his abode.

Though Sri Rama was also one of the Incarnations of Lord Vishnu, He had lived in Ayodhya thousands of years before Sri Krishna's lifetime. Yet Hanuman, the great devotee of Lord Rama, did not doubt that Lord Rama and Sita could appear in Dwaraka, even though the all-knowing Hanuman was fully aware of the fact that Krishna was the Lord of Dwaraka. Certainly Hanuman knew that no one except Krishna could manifest Rama Bhava. What really happened was that Hanuman was determined to use this opportunity to see his Lord with Sita in human form once again. Lord Krishna, the servant of His devotees, happily fulfilled His great devotee's wish and blessed him. Only a Purna Avatara can become one with any other God or Goddess. Being such an Avatara, Krishna easily manifested Rama Bhava. One day, Lord Krishna asked His wives including Satyabhama, one of His dear ones, to assume Sita Bhava, but none were able to. Finally Rukmini, an Incarnation of Goddess Lakshmi, effortlessly assumed Sita Bhava.

In the case of an Avesa Avatara, godly powers enter into a particular person and withdraw after fulfilling the intended goal. This was not the case with Sri Krishna and Rukmini. What Lord

Krishna did was to manifest Rama Bhava or the attributes of Rama which were already potential in Him.

There is a similar incident in the life of Lord Chaitanya of Bengal. One day Pandit Srivasa, an ardent devotee of Lord Narasimha, was performing his usual chanting (mantra japa), while sitting in his family shrine room. Suddenly there was a knock on the door. "Who is that?" the pandit asked. "Behold the Beloved Deity whom you are worshipping," came the reply. Pandit Srivasa opened the door and beheld Lord Chaitanya standing before him on the threshold of the house in a divine mood. He entered the shrine room and sat on the seat which was specially made for worship. The pandit saw the Lord Narasimha shining within Lord Chaitanya and with great devotion worshipped Him in Lord Chaitanya's form. Lord Chaitanya blessed the pundit's family by permitting all of them to take part in the worship.

After everyone had received his blessings, Lord Chaitanya fell unconscious. On regaining his external awareness after a few moments, he asked the pandit, "What happened? I cannot remember anything. Did I say anything wrong?" With all humility, Srivasa prostrated before his Lord and said, "O Bhagavan, please do not delude this humble servant of Yours anymore. By Your Grace I was able to see who You are!" Hearing this, Lord Chaitanya graciously smiled in a gesture of confirmation. Many such incidents in Lord Chaitanya's life reveal that he gave darshan to his devotees in diverse bhavas.

From these illustrations one can clearly glimpse what Bhava Darshan is. Bhava Darshan is the manifestation of different Isvara Bhavas or Divine Moods by an Incarnation of God according to the wishes of the devotees. Anandamayi Ma, who lived in Bengal, used to manifest Krishna and Kali Bhavas while singing bhajans. These Bhavas manifested by Incarnations took place only on certain occasions to fulfil a particular end, especially in response to the ardent desire of their devotees. Moreover, they would last only for a short time. The Holy Mother Amritanandamayi manifests the Divine Moods three nights a week lasting for long periods of 10 to 12 hours depending upon the number of devotees present for Darshan. This is the Holy Mother's way of serving humanity, plunged as it is in the deep quagmire of worldliness.

Lord Chaitanya is said to have had two bhavas, that of a devotee, in which mood he was most frequently seen, and Bhagavat Bhava, during which he would reveal his real state of Self-Abidance. Sri Ramakrishna Paramahamsa also revealed more than one bhava. It is said that he even developed a small growth like a tail during the period of his spiritual practices in Hanuman Bhava.

During the Holy Mother's Krishna and Devi Bhavas, she brings out That which is within her and manifests those Divine Beings in order to bless her devotees. The Holy Mother once said regarding the bhavas:

"Mother is not manifesting even an infinitesimal part of her spiritual power during the Bhavas. If it were to be manifested as it is, no one could come near!" She continues, "All the deities of the Hindu Pantheon, who represent the numberless aspects of the One Supreme Being, exist within us. A Divine Incarnation can manifest any of them by mere will for the good of the world. Krishna Bhava is the manifestation of the Purusha or Pure Being aspect, and Devi Bhava is the manifestation of the Eternal Feminine, the Creatrix, the active principle of the Impersonal Absolute. Here is a crazy girl who puts on the garb of Krishna and after some time that of Devi, but it is within this crazy girl that both exist. However, it should be remembered that all objects having a name or form are mere mental projections. Why decorate an elephant? Why should a lawyer wear a black coat or why does a policeman wear a uniform and a cap? All these are merely external aids meant to create a certain impression. In a like manner, Mother dons the garb of Krishna and Devi in order to give strength to the devotional attitude of the people coming for Darshan. The Atman or Self that is in me is also within you. If you can realize that Indivisible Principle that is ever shining in you, you will become That."

Even now some people believe that Lord Krishna and Devi visit the Holy Mother's body three nights a week, after which They leave her body. This misconception springs from a lack of correct understanding about the Holy Mother's Divine Moods. These Divine Bhavas are nothing but the external revelation of her incessant Oneness with the Supreme. They have nothing to do with possession or Divine Grace as it is commonly understood.

Answering the queries of the devotees, the Holy Mother has explained many points relating to the Bhavas:

Devotee: Many devotees say that Mother is the same during the Divine Bhavas and at other times. If this is so, then what is the significance of the Bhavas?

Mother: During the time of the Bhava Darshan Mother will remove two or three layers (veils, so to say), so that the devotees can obtain a glimpse of the Supreme. Different people have different kinds of belief. Mother's intention is to somehow help the people approach God. Some are interested only if they see Mother in the costume of Devi or Krishna. Not only that... very few people know anything about spirituality. Some people find it difficult to believe Mother's words during ordinary times, but if Mother says the same thing during the Devi Bhava they will believe.

Devotee: Mother, is there any particular time for manifesting this Bhava?

Mother: No, there is not. It can be manifested at any time. Mere will is enough.

Devotee: Mother, why do you wear these costumes of Krishna and Devi?

Mother: It will help the people to remember what Bhava is. Child, each attire is important in its own way. We are naked when we are born. Later, according to each country and social custom, people adopt different kinds of dress. Whatever the dress, the person is the same. In this age people give much importance to dress. Mother will make this point clear through an anecdote. One man was cutting down a tree which was growing by the side of a road. Another man who happened to see him doing this said, "Don't cut down that tree! It is wrong to do so, it is against the law." The man not only refused to stop cutting but also scolded him severely. The person who tried to prevent the hooligan from cutting the tree was a policeman. He departed but soon returned in his official dress. Even from a distance the mere sight of the policeman's cap was enough to make the hooligan flee without looking back. See the different impact created when he came in ordinary and then official dress. Therefore, special attire is needed to teach ignorant people. Likewise, the costumes of Krishna and Devi Bhavas. Some people who still feel dissatisfied even after talking to Mother for hours will feel fully content after conversing with her only for a couple of seconds during Bhava Darshan. They feel peaceful after having told all their worries directly to God.

All Incarnations are unique in nature. One cannot say that Krishna was greater than Rama or that Rama was greater than Buddha. Each of Them had Their own task to fulfil and adopted befitting ways to uplift humanity. But this does not mean that They had different visions of life. Their actions cannot be assessed using the measuring rod of our limited intellect and logic. We can get perhaps a glimpse of their greatness through pure intuition born of spiritual practice. The spiritual experiences gained by thousands of devotees through the Holy Mother throws much light on this Great Soul's inexplicable spiritual power. In the following pages we will share with the reader some of the divine experiences of the Holy Mother's devotees as related by them.

Chapter Twelve

Experiences of Spiritual Aspirants

Unnikrishnan (Swami Turiyamritananda Puri)

Unnikrishnan was the first person to be fortunate enough to meet Mother and stay with her for a long time. He did not continue his schooling after the sixth grade. In him we see a wonderful example of the Mother's kindness and grace. With the Guru's Grace, even a semiliterate young boy can become an inspiring poet. Unnikrishna's life is testimony to this.

After completing his brief schooling, the young Unni wandered freely, engaging himself in a variety of activities. In 1976, when he was twenty years old, he heard about the Holy Mother and came to see her. He felt great faith and devotion for Amma from that very first meeting. Thereafter, he visited her frequently, seeking her instructions. A year had passed when one day Mother asked him to stay with her in order to perform the daily worship in the temple. She instructed him to chant the Lalita Sahasranama (the Thousand Names of the Divine Mother) every day.

From then on his life took a dramatic turn. The mere presence of the Holy Mother inspired him with a strong desire to realize the Truth. His days were filled with the practice of austere penance, formal worship, conversations with Amma, reading of scriptures, and other spiritual activities. As a result of this disciplined way of life, he gradually realised that the glorious Mother of the Bhava Darshan, and the sweet Mother in her more usual moods were, in fact, one and the same, two facets or manifestations of the same infinite Divine Power, played out for the good of the world. This insight greatly stimulated his desire to perform sadhana, (spiritual practices), and he surrendered himself fully at Mother's feet, regarding her as his sole support in life. As time passed, his spiritual disciplines took an even more rigorous turn; he came to eat, sleep and speak less. On occasion, he fasted for several weeks at a stretch. He used to sleep on the bare ground without so much as a blanket to cover himself during the winter and the rainy season. When he went on pilgrimage, as he occasionally did, he travelled on foot the whole way, without recourse to any vehicle.

One day, with tears in his eyes, he asked Mother with over-flowing emotion, "Who is my real Mother?" Regarding him with great tenderness, the Holy Mother took his head on her lap and replied, "My child, you are my son, and I am your mother." Unnikrishnan was overwhelmed with inexpressible bliss welling up from within. As he silently gazed at Mother's radiant face, he wept with joy.

By the infinite Grace of the Mother, Unnikrishnan has become a prolific poet whose works are pregnant with philosophical truth and devotional sweetness. Once, when his parents had sent some relatives to bring him back home, he replied with the following poignant verse:

Having left my home long ago,
If I were now to lead a worldly life, would I gain

Peace of mind thereby?
What profit has there been in such an existence
Even from time immemorial?

When I am struggling to free myself
From the utter folly of the world,
Why do you pave a fool's path straight
To the servitude of the beggar?
Can I ever agree to such a fate?

Unni describes his first meeting with Mother in the following evocative way:

Akalatta kovilil

In a distant temple a glowing flame burnt
Without getting extinguished.
The Mother with infinite compassion was
Seated there as a guiding light for those
Wandering destitute in the darkness.

One day while I wandered there,
That embodiment of mercy called me aside.
Opening the inner sanctum
She dabbed sandalwood paste on my forehead.

Melodiously singing the exalted praises of the Lord,
She made a place for me on Her soft and Sacred arm.
Coming near, a wondrous divine
Dream whispered this truth in my ear:
"What need is there for tears? Don't you know
That you have come near the Mother of the Universe?"
With a sigh I awoke, Her Lotus Face
Indelibly impressed on my consciousness.

Once when Unnikrishnan experienced some inner conflict, he fasted for several weeks. When the Holy Mother learned of it, she also stopped eating and drinking. Unni, unaware of her fasting, continued his vow. After a couple of days, while doing his daily worship, the Holy Mother's father scolded him for not taking food and thereby making Mother starve. Soon after the worship was over, he came to the doorway of Mother's hut with a heavy heart and eyes filled with tears. Calling him to her side, she caressed him with great love and looking at his shivering body said, "Unni, my son, if you are feeling some inner agitation, you should come tell Mother about it. Don't torture your body like this. To do tapas, the body is needed. Eat at least for the sustenance of the body." Saying this, she asked for a plate of rice and fed Unni with her own hands, eating out of the same plate herself.

A few months after his settling in the ashram, Unni, who had the temperament of a wandering mendicant, decided to go away. Without informing anyone, he made ready for his journey. As he was about to depart on a Darshan night, a man suddenly came to him with Mother's counsel, "Mother says that even though you are getting ready to go, you should not depart now." Unable to disobey the Holy Mother, he cancelled his journey. Once more some time later he tried to leave, but the same thing happened. Finally, he did actually leave, but had to return after two days. He thereby became convinced that without Mother's knowledge and blessings, he could do nothing.

Mother once said that "Unni's songs spring from his meditation." What greater recognition could there be? The following is a translation of two of his songs:

I have wandered in distant lands carrying a
Heavy burden of sorrow. At last, coming to You
I have surrendered myself at Your Lotus Feet.
O Mother, won't You kindly wash away my

Endless afflictions and tears with the waters of
Your Love?

Consider not this poor one as a sinner as no one
Else is there in this world as my stay and support.
O Embodiment of Compassion, please caress
Me with the Moonlight of Your beautiful eyes.

O Mother, throwing away this heavy burden of
Thoughts let me sit near You and merge in Meditation.
O You who are described in the Vedas and Vedanta! O
Mother of all the Gods and Goddesses! Won't You fulfil
this wish springing from my Soul to gain the Supreme
Self?

O Mother, when will that time come when I will
renounce all taste for pleasure-seeking and become one
with Your Holy Feet?

Balu (Swami Amritaswarupananda Puri)

Balu tells of the following experiences of Mother's Grace:
"When my B.A. final examinations were over, I heard about
a girl endowed with supernatural powers, who appeared in the
forms of Devi and Krishna. Though my faith in the existence of
God was deep-rooted, I was not much interested in seeing her.
Some of my relatives and friends, who had visited her, spoke
very highly of her and continued to press me to visit her ashram.
Finally, with a skeptical mind, I came to the ashram one evening, accompanied by my uncle. As I approached the grounds,
the melody of a moving devotional song sounded in my ears,
capturing my attention. Approaching a small shrine, I saw a girl

in white clothes singing songs poignant with love and devotion. Listening to her song, I could see that her heart was overflowing with divine bliss and love. The vibrations of her singing pierced my heart, evoking the most tender feelings.

When my turn came, I entered the shrine room where she was seated on a peetham or stool. I prostrated before her, and when I got up, she took hold of my hand and looked into my eyes. Her eyes were beaming like the full moon. That look penetrated me; that smile bound me and made me motionless. Infinite compassion manifested on her face. Slowly she put my head on her shoulder and softly but emphatically said, 'Child, I am your mother and you are my child.' That sweet voice entered deep into my heart and I became enraptured with inexplicable joy. This is what I had been searching for! I burst into tears. Love in all its purity, Motherhood in its universal essence had assumed a form. Thrilled by this experience, I sat near Mother the whole night.

When I reached home the next day, I realised the great change which had taken place in me. I became totally indifferent to all my usual activities. My desire to see her again intensified. All my thoughts were fixed on her. That night I was unable to sleep. Whenever I tried to close my eyes, the Mother appeared in front of me. The next day I returned to the ashram. After the second meeting with Mother, my desire to break off the fetters of worldliness became still more intense. Thinking of the Mother, I became like a madman. I forgot to eat, to sleep and to take bath. I abandoned my fancy way of dressing and combing my hair. My parents and other family members were worried by the change in me and forbade me from going to Vallickavu.

The next day after participating in the bhajan, I entered the shrine with this resolve: 'Mother, if I am your child, please accept me.' Placing my head on her shoulder, Mother lovingly said, 'Son, when Mother heard you singing, she understood that this voice is meant to merge in God. At that moment Mother came to you and made you one with her. You are my very own.'

One night when I was half asleep, I smelled a peculiar sweet fragrance pervading the room. I opened my eyes and found that the fragrance was real, not just a dream or imagination. Suddenly, I felt someone's hands stroking my forehead. I looked up and to my astonishment I saw Mother standing at the end of the cot above my head. I couldn't believe my eyes. She smiled at me and said, 'My son, Mother is always with you, don't worry.' Saying this, she disappeared.

Next morning I rushed to Vallickavu, but Mother was not there. She returned only at four in the afternoon. Without a word, she ran to the house and emerged with a plate of rice which she fed me as a mother would her son. While feeding me she said, 'Last night, Mother came to you.' Overwhelmed with happiness, I cried like a small child. I had not in fact eaten anything yet that day.

After Mother initiated me with a mantra, I was unable to stay at home. My yearning to live in her presence and to seek her instructions increased day by day. Disregarding all the obstacles my relatives created, I left home and joined the residents of the Ashram.

Two years later, as we were sitting in a devotee's house, she suddenly said to me, 'My son Balu, you must get a Master's degree in philosophy.' I had previously told Mother that I was not going to continue my studies, but just wanted to be absorbed in thinking about her. Now, two years later, she was asking me to study again. From my experience, I knew that she would not say or do anything without a purpose, so I enrolled in the graduate program. Now a real problem arose; who would teach me? I would have to prepare eight papers, four on Indian philosophy, with which I was somewhat familiar, and four on Western philosophy, which was an entirely new subject for me. I asked Mother where I was to find some one to teach me.

'Don't worry about it. Someone will come here to instruct you. Wait patiently and see,' she said. But I was restless and frequently disturbed her with the same question. A week later, a devotee directed me to a man who was a philosophy professor. I went to see him to explain my predicament. He was willing to teach me, but refused to come to the ashram. I tried to make him understand my difficulty in leaving the ashram to study. At last he agreed to visit the ashram but said, 'I cannot stay there or give you classes there. If you want to study, you must come to my house. If not, drop the matter right now .' I thought that since I had no other choice, l would let him at least come to the ashram to see Mother.

The following Thursday I went to fetch him from his home. When we reached the ashram, I invited him to come see Mother, but he refused. When Mother sat for her usual singing before the Bhava Darshan, he was watching from a distance. Even after the Darshan began, he continued to observe from a distance. I approached him to suggest that, if he liked, he could go inside the temple and have Mother's Darshan. 'No, I have never prostrated to anyone before. I don't want to do that,' he replied. I left him alone and sat down to sing. A few minutes later I saw him rush into the temple and heard a loud cry. He had fallen flat in front of Mother and was weeping like a small child. An hour or two passed. Coming out of the shrine, he called me aside and said, 'She is a Great Soul indeed! Every week I will come here to teach you.' Thus, Mother herself arranged a teacher for me.

Making references to various books, the professor dictated a lot of notes to me, but didn't explain anything. Unfortunately, for various reasons, we were not able to continue the course of study regularly, and Western philosophy still remained an unknown subject to me. Only three months were left before the examinations. The professor dictated some more notes to me and gave me a summary of the whole thing. As I was involved in different activities of the ashram and was frequently travelling with Mother, I could not follow through with my studies. Now only one month remained before the exams. Mother asked me to write all eight papers in one sitting. I was really worried how I could possibly write both the first and final year papers together. I dedicated the project to Mother's feet and began reading. At last it was the day before my departure to Tirupati, (a town in Andhra Pradesh, seven hundred miles from the ashram), where I had registered my name in the University as a student of philosophy.

At noon I was about to pack my things. Suddenly, I heard Mother calling me from her room. I ran to her room and saw her packing some things in a bag. She put the last item into it and closed it. Another big bag stood ready on her table. With great affection she announced, 'Son, I have packed everything for your journey.' Pointing to the bag on the table she said, 'That bag contains dhotis, shirts, towels, two blankets and other clothes, and in this one there is coconut oil, soap, a mirror, comb, something to make a hot drink and other useful things. I have packed all these things so you might save time for your studies.' I was stunned. I simply gazed at her loving face. My heart was overflowing with joy. My eyes filled with tears and I broke down weeping.

This was the first time that I was going to be away from her, and it would be for an entire month. My heart was very heavy. In the train I sat in a corner to hide my tears. All the passengers were chatting cheerfully, but my mind was full of sorrow to be separated from Mother. Throughout the trip, I thought of nothing but her. The following morning I reached Tirupati. My days were filled with excruciating pain of separation. I felt like a fish out of water. I tried to concentrate on my studies, but failed.

Each minute passed at a snail's pace. I was even unable to look at Mother's picture. Each object brought from the ashram reminded me of Mother and her gracious form. I forgot to eat and sleep. Each day dragged like a year for me. Now and then I collapsed. Unable to bear the separation, I burst into tears. By the time the final exams began, I somehow managed to write the papers. There was nobody to share my sorrow.

At that time, I received a letter from Mother. Several times I read and reread it. Soaked by my tears, the letter turned wet. Mother's letter to me read:

Darling Son,

Your Mother is always with you. Son, Mother doesn't feel that you are away from her. My child, Mother can see your yearning heart. Mother can hear your cries. My son, this world is so beautiful. The flowers, the vast ocean, the chirping birds, the expanse of the sky, trees, bushes, forests, mountains and valleys are all here. God made this earth beautiful. See Him in everything. Love Him in all beings. Cut open the bond separating you from God. Let your mind flow ceaselessly toward Him. Son, nothing is bad in this world. Everything is good. See the good and virtuous part. Let your mental flower blossom and spread its fragrance all around.

That night I was sitting outside my room watching the trees and plants dancing in the gentle breeze. The sky was full of glittering stars, and the silver light of the moon flooded the earth with splendour. I thought, 'This breeze may blow to my Mother; it may be fortunate enough to caress my Mother's body. Yes, no doubt this is carrying my dear Mother's divine fragrance. If I had wings, I would fly to my Mother.' The following poem was written that night:

Tarapathangale

O stars, can't you please come down?
Mother is here to sing a lullaby to you.
She is the stream of never-ending love and
She is the shade-giving tree for seeking minds.
O cool gentle breeze who comes slowly humming
Silent songs in the night, what did you whisper so
Sweetly in my ears? The sweet stories of my Mother?

The sun and moon slowly rise and set
In the blue sky every day.
Don't you have the desire to see my
Mother who has given you this divine splendour?
Trees and creepers grow in abundance in
The silent lonely valleys and hillsides.
As if to console me their tender branches dance in the
wind.

I was in an intense and unusual mood. I paced the floor like one gone mad. Somehow I controlled myself and decided to leave the next day. I had one more paper to write. I decided not to appear for the first year exams, which were to begin in four days. I thought, 'Mother has asked me to attend all the exams, but this time I am going to act against her advice.'

Finally I decided to seek Mother's permission in a peculiar way. I took three pieces of paper of equal size. On the first piece I wrote, 'Son, you come back.' On the second one I wrote, 'You write all the papers and then come,' and on the third I wrote, 'As my son likes.' I rolled all three papers in the same manner, shook them, and took Mother's picture from the bag. With this prayer I humbly offered the papers to her, 'O Mother, I am going to take one of these papers. Let me know your will, whatever it be.' With closed eyes, I took one of the papers with trembling hands. I opened it. Alas! it was the one on which I had written, 'You write all the papers and then come.' Not satisfied with the first attempt, I tried my lot again with three more pieces of paper ,but again I picked the same note. My mind, however, was so yearning to see Mother that I finally decided to leave the next day.

The next day, after attending the last of the final exams, I rushed to pack my things and was about to leave. Suddenly I noticed some things lying in the corner of the room. They were some useless newspapers, which I had used as a wrapper to bring things from the Ashram, and a broken piece of a soap box. I thought, 'How intense was my pain when I was separated from Mother. Perhaps these things, too, share that pain; if I leave them here, it will be a sin.' I carefully packed those things as well in my bag.

The following day I reached the ashram. On the way to Mother's room, I saw my brother, Venu. Astonished, he said, 'Last night Mother told me that you are getting very restless and that you will come today.' I entered Mother's room and fell at her feet crying. Mother lifted me up and consoled me saying 'Son, I know your heart. This love is good, but try to acquire more mental strength. A sadhak should be soft like a flower and hard like a diamond. You must go and write the other papers. Even if you fail, Mother won't mind. Tomorrow you go and come back when the exams are over.'

The next morning I went back to Tirupati. After a week when the last exam was over, I returned to the ashram. I was not satisfied with my answers and even feared that I might fail. Mother calmly said, 'Forget about it. Don't doubt. You will succeed.' When the results were published, I was surprised to see that I had passed with a high second class. Simply to be in the presence of the Holy Mother is a tapas. There is always something new and fresh. Every moment one experiences enlightening insights which lead the devotee through different realms of spirituality, evolving him from one plane to the next. In the beginning stages of my spiritual life, I sometimes used to feel that I had understood the Holy Mother. Later I realised that I had understood nothing about Mother at all."

Venu (Swami Pranavamritananda Puri)

Venu is Balu's brother. They were both infants when their mother died. After her death, Balu grew up in his father's house, and Venu was raised by his aunt, Saraswathy Amma, in a religious and spiritual atmosphere. Venu was the pet of the family and never experienced the loss of a mother's love and affection. After completing secondary school at age fifteen, Venu moved to his father's house to continue his education at a local college. Though he manifested an inclination towards spirituality at an early age, during his college years he led a worldly life. Even then, whenever he saw a devotional movie or a monk in ochre robes, he would feel again the stirrings of his dormant spiritual impulse.

By the time Venu was in college, his brother Balu had already met the Holy Mother and had dedicated himself to spirituality. Though Balu told his brother about the Holy Mother several times, Venu paid little attention. Moreover, he openly scorned the Holy Mother and asserted, "I won't come near that fishergirl." Nevertheless, even before meeting Venu, Amma predicted to Balu, "Your brother also is my son. He, too, will come here." Hearing this, Balu was worried because there was already an uproar in his family over his own decision to leave home and the worldly life. What would happen if Venu also followed in his footsteps? However, the Divine Will is supreme, beyond the realm of ordinary mortal vision. What was destiny would inevitably come to pass.

While Venu was studying for the final year of his Bachelor of Science degree, the Holy Mother visited his aunt's house. When Venu arrived that day, the Holy Mother was standing on the verandah of the house. Without even looking at her, Venu strode past Mother into his room where Sreekumar and some other residents of Mother's Ashram were seated.

Suddenly and unexpectedly, the Holy Mother approached Venu and, holding his hands like a loving mother, said, "Aren't you my son Balu's brother? Mother has been yearning to see you." Venu's heart melted, and he realised in a flash that Mother was not an ordinary personality, but rather a fountain of motherly love and tenderness. Venu felt attracted to her as a piece of iron is drawn to a magnet. In the afternoon when Amma fed everyone, Venu also got a ball of rice. He was profoundly affected to see her infinite love, equal vision and childlike innocence. Her face was radiant and overflowing with spiritual radiance. Her lucid way of explaining spiritual mysteries, ecstatic and bewitching bhajans, and above all her absolute humility impressed him deeply. Within a short period of time, Venu found himself being drawn to the Mother. Even when the Holy Mother was talking to others, it seemed to Venu that she was actually responding to the doubts which had cropped up in his mind.

The first meeting with the Holy Mother left a deep impression in Venu's mind, and all the prejudices which he had had about the Holy Mother and spiritual life vanished. Each day his longing to see the Mother increased. At last in February, 1980, he came to Vallickavu. When Venu saw the Mother he burst into tears. The Holy Mother caught hold of him and made him sit near her. That night, when Venu went into the temple during Krishna Bhava, he felt that he was standing before Lord Sri Krishna Himself. His mind overflowed with joy and he could neither cry nor laugh. He prayed to Mother to bless him by bestowing pure devotion and knowledge on him. Mother said, "Son, you will get what you are seeking." Mother gave him a mantra written on a piece of paper and a garland of tulasi leaves.

After Venu's first meeting with the Holy Mother, he lost all desire to continue his studies; his only wish was to lead a spiritual life. On the Mother's insistence, Venu prepared for his college examinations which were a month away. Professors and students were amazed to see Venu coming to the college with a completely shaven head and sacred ashes on his forehead. They thought he had gone mad. His mind was entirely immersed in the thought of the Holy Mother. Indeed, he was so focused on her that he inadvertently prepared for the following day's examination, not for that day's paper. Somehow he did manage to complete the exams and came to stay with the Holy Mother in September, 1980.

One day in connection with a festival, sweet pudding was prepared in the ashram. It was customary to offer it to God before distributing it among the devotees. Venu took a tumblerful and placed it in the small shrine before the temple. Finding nothing else to cover the tumbler with, and looking around to make sure that Mother was not nearby, he plucked a tender leaf from a small plant growing near the shrine. Mother noticed the act from a distance and called aloud, 'Hey Venu!' Hearing Mother's voice, he tried to hide the tender leaf, but in his haste he tipped the tumbler spilling the entire contents on the sand. By this time, Venu was completely undone, and, hoping to escape further notice, he scooped up the pudding from the sand and stuffed it back into the tumbler, knowing that it was wrong to put it back in the shrine.

Mother, who was observing the whole scene from a distance, approached him and said in a serious tone, "Son, even a dog won't eat this. What of human beings? Then how could you offer it to God? Son, will you eat it? No! This is a real sin. God will accept anything that is offered to Him with pure love and devotion, not caring what it is. He only sees the attitude behind the offering. If you were really ignorant of your deed, I would not have minded it, but with full knowledge that what you were doing was wrong, you proceeded to do it. Not only that. You have committed another error by plucking a tender leaf from that small plant. How merciless you are! I can see the plant crying in pain. If someone pinches you, how much pain you suffer. Son, even though you don't feel its pain, Mother does."

Venu realised his mistake and repented. He prayed for forgiveness. Mother said, "Son, whatever errors you commit, I take to be some fault of my own. Mother is not at all angry with you, but in order to lead you on the path to Perfection, she has to pretend to be so."

Venu says, "Nothing can be concealed from the Holy Mother. She knows everything. About five years ago I had an experience which illustrates this fact. One night during supper while everyone was eating kanji (rice gruel), I suddenly had a strong desire to have some mango pickles as a side dish. I had seen them in the ashram kitchen earlier in the day but, as they were meant for the labourers and visiting devotees, we residents were not supposed to take them. Also, Mother had told us that, as spiritual aspirants, we should not eat things which were very spicy, sour, salty or sweet. She would often come into the kitchen unannounced to see whether her instructions were being followed. Although I was fully aware of this, the desire for the pickles got the better of me.

Without making any noise, I entered the kitchen and stealthily stole two big slices of mango pickle. I was about to leave when suddenly I heard Mother's voice, 'Venu, what is in your hand?' I was shocked and, to avoid being caught red-handed, I threw the mango slices away. Mother then searched and found the slices;

seizing me, she caught hold of my hands and tied them to a post. I was ashamed and full of fear."

Seeing his childlike fear and innocence, Mother burst into laughter. Actually, the Holy Mother was enjoying looking upon Venu as the child Krishna who was tied to a mortar by His mother, Yashoda, for stealing butter and milk from the Gopis' houses. After a couple of seconds, Mother untied him and lovingly served him some mango pickles. She said, "Son, only if the taste of the tongue is controlled can one enjoy the taste of the heart."

Mother has her own ways to exhaust the negative tendencies of her spiritual children. Sometimes she says, "I am a crazy girl who knows nothing." She pretends that she is an ignorant, innocent village girl, but her eyes penetrate the truth of everything. Once the mistake is detected, then the Great Teacher in her rises up and instructs the student befittingly, as she temporarily conceals her Motherhood.

Sreekumar (Swami Purnamritananda Puri)

Sreekumar was an electronic engineer before coming to her. While studying for his B.A. in 1979, he heard about a woman who could assume divine moods and bless devotees in various ways according to their particular problems. Though believing in God, he doubted that Divinity could manifest through a human being. Observing the nature of this world where few are happy and the majority suffer, his faith waned in a beneficent God. Finally he decided to see for himself whether or not the Holy Mother possessed divine power.

With a skeptical mind, he came to the ashram in March, 1979, and entered the shrine room, drawing close to the Holy Mother. Her loving and compassionate glance entered deep into

Sreekumar's heart. Her mere presence transported him to another world where God, His Holy Name, and he himself alone existed and he became oblivious to his surroundings. This experience bound him to Mother, and his mind became filled with the thought of her alone.

About his second meeting with the Holy Mother Sreekumar says, "I heard some people calling her 'child' (kunju) while others called her 'Mother' (Amma). After Bhava Darshan, she talked with the devotees. All of a sudden, she would behave like a small and innocent child. She would play with the devotees, and seeing her innocent ways, their hearts would rejoice, forgetting everything else. Sometimes she would sing and dance and the next moment, while hearing a song, she would weep and sit motionless as if lost to the world. Some bowed down before her and others kissed her hand; still others sang devotional songs. Then, like one gone mad, she would roll on the ground and laugh." In the beginning, Sreekumar felt that Mother was being temporarily possessed by the Divine Mother Kali and also by Krishna, but gradually, in close association with her, he came to understand that she was actually manifesting her inner identity with the Supreme Reality.

Sreekumar's relationship with the Holy Mother strengthened day by day. It became very difficult for him to be away from her. Whenever he could get time, he would spend it with the Holy Mother. Sometimes the Holy Mother would feed him with her own hands and would give him spiritual instructions at the same time. One day she asked him, "Has Mother given you a mantra to repeat?" He replied, "Yes, it was written on a small piece of paper and given for the improvement of my studies." Mother then told him, "Son, during Devi Bhava, Mother will initiate you." That night, Sreekumar was initiated with a mantra. From that moment he decided to dedicate his life to spirituality under the Holy Mother's guidance.

Although Sreekumar's parents were devoted to the Holy Mother, they did not approve of his becoming a monk. Their objection was mainly that his father was retired and his sister still remained to be married. They therefore arranged a job for him in Bangalore, about six hundred kilometres away. On days when his breaking heart yearned painfully for her presence, he would see a vision of her. In order to console him, Mother used to send him occasional letters. It was at this time that he wrote the following song:

Arikil undenkilum

O Mother, even though You are near,
I am wandering, unable to know You.

Even though I have eyes
I am searching, unable to see You.
Are You the beautiful moon
That blooms forth in the blue winter night?
I am the wave that, unable to reach the sky
Beats its head against the shore.

When I came to understand the truth
That all worldly comforts are worthless,
I longed to know You,
Shedding tears day and night.

Won't You come to comfort me
Who am weary of the burden of sorrow?
With the desire that You will come
I am waiting always.

His intense desire to see the Holy Mother and to stay with her led Sreekumar to return home, even before the end of his first month in Bangalore. Laid up with fever, he was hospitalized immediately upon arriving home. His longing to see the Mother continued to increase until one morning at four a.m. he had a wonderful experience. "My father had gone out to get some coffee for me. I was alone in the room when all of a sudden my hands and legs felt paralysed. A cool, gentle breeze caressed me, and to my great surprise, I saw Mother entering the room. With a benign smile on her face, she walked toward me. Like a small child, I started crying. She then sat beside me and put my head on her lap. She didn't say anything. I was overcome with emotion. Words stuck in my throat. An effulgence from Mother's body flooded the room and she was surrounded by a divine light. At that moment, the door opened and my father walked in. The Holy Mother immediately vanished."

A few days later, Mother visited Sreekumar's house in the morning. She was sitting in front of the house playing with some children. All of a sudden, she got up and walked through the fields towards the east with her hands forming a mudra. After walking some distance, she entered a forest grove where a certain family had been worshipping snakes. In a semiconscious mood and with half-closed eyes, she cast a bewitching smile on the family and sat on the small shrine built for the snake worship. Several people gathered to see this unusual sight. However, others were afraid to enter the forest which was known for poisonous snakes. Hearing the news, the owners of the grove also came and stood before Mother with joined palms.

They asked, "Mother, we are doing the worship without a break. Do we need to do anything more?" Mother replied, "Keep a glass of fresh water here daily. That will suffice." When the Holy Mother came back to the house, the family asked her, "Mother, what made you go there?" She replied, "Worship of snakes has been going on there for a very long time. Mother went there to satisfy the desire of the presiding deities in that forest. From the moment that I arrived here, I had the feeling that they were beckoning me."

Shortly after this, Sreekumar's parents found him a job in Bombay. They insisted so firmly that finally Sreekumar had no other choice but to go there. With great reluctance he left for Bombay, once more separated from the Holy Mother. While travelling in the train, he felt the presence of the Holy Mother intensely. In a half-waking, half-sleeping state he enjoyed constant visions of her and revelled in the bliss of her Divine Presence. Finally, after eight months he was unable to bear the separation from her any longer and submitted his resignation to his employer.

During his stay in Bombay, Sreekumar wrote this poem which reveals his aching heart:

Azhikulil

The sun has set in the western ocean
And the day has started its lament...
It is but the play of the Universal Architect.
So why should you, O closing lotuses, be dejected?

This world, full of misery and sorrow
Is but a drama of God, and I, the onlooker,
Am but a wooden puppet in His hands
Having no tears to shed.

Like a flame, my mind is burning in
Separation from You in this ocean of grief.
I am getting tossed about,
Unable to find the shore.

Even before coming to Mother to take up spiritual life seriously, Sreekumar used to have experiences in the astral plane of existence. While lying down, he would feel his subtle body emerge from his gross body and travel around. During such moments, even though his eyes were closed, he could clearly see the objective world.

During his stay in Bombay, he had a thrilling experience. It was daytime and he was relaxing with his eyes closed after meditation. Suddenly, his body became stiff. He felt his subtle form separate from the gross one and immediately heard a thundering sound, followed by an outpouring of billows of smoke into the atmosphere in the midst of which he beheld the figure of the Holy Mother dressed in the colourful costume which she wears during Devi Bhava. The magnificent figure of the Holy Mother filled his mind with awe and reverence. A few minutes passed as he beheld this sublime vision, unable to move or open his eyes.

On the evening of the twenty-eighth of January, 1980, Sreekumar was about to go to his house to visit his parents when Mother stopped him saying, "Stay here; don't go anywhere today." In his own words, "I was happy to hear Mother's words and cancelled my plans to go out. At around six o'clock in the evening I was standing outside talking to some people when suddenly something bit me on the leg. I cried out in pain hearing which Mother came running to the spot. Immediately finding the wound, Mother sucked out the blood and poison and then spat it out. In spite of this, the pain became unbearable. Seeing me rolling in agony due to the excruciating pain, Mother tried to comfort me. Finally, due to the insistence of others, she allowed me to be taken to a doctor specializing in snake bites. The doctor told, 'The snake which has bitten you was an extremely poisonous one but strangely enough the poison does not seem to have affected your body or blood.' By Mother's loving and affectionate care, I at last fell asleep at three a.m. only after which Mother herself retired.

The next morning Mother told me, 'Son, wherever you might have been, you were destined to be bitten by a snake. However, as it happened in Mother's presence, nothing serious has come of it. That is why Mother prevented you from going away from here yesterday.' Later, after reaching my house, I went through my horoscope and was surprised to find that something had been written therein concerning that would-be fatal incident. It said, 'At the age of twenty-two there is the probability of poisoning. Therefore, special worship and offerings in the temple should be made for good health'."

By the Grace of the Holy Mother, Sreekumar had several spiritual experiences which always served as a source of inspiration for him to continue his sadhana with more and more enthusiasm. After making some provision for his parents and sister, he came to settle permanently at the ashram.

Ramakrishnan (Swami Ramakrishnananda Puri)

Ramakrishnan is the son of brahmana parents from Palghat in Kerala. In 1978, when he was an employee of the State Bank of Travancore, he heard about the Holy Mother from one of his friends. One evening he and his friend came to see her. Though brought up in an orthodox family, Ramakrishnan was heading for trouble, falling under the influence of bad company in college. When he saw the Holy Mother, he burst into tears. All his inner coarseness melted and softened until everything was washed away in those purifying tears. After this, he would come for almost all the Darshans in order to see Mother in the Divine Mood. He would cry like a small child and pray to her to give him the vision of Madurai Meenakshi, his beloved Deity. He would even fast on certain days in deep sorrow for having failed to gain that vision. On those days , the Holy Mother would feed him with sweet pudding without even mentioning his fast. Weeping with intense yearning while lying on Mother's lap during Devi Bhava, he would ask her, "Mother, will you come to me tomorrow? At least let me hear the jingling of your anklets." Mother granted his humble prayers, giving him many visions of his beloved Deity. Some days he would hear the jingling of Mother's anklets and see the Divine Mother; at other times he would smell a divine fragrance pervading the atmosphere around him.

There were two significant events which inspired Ramakrishnan to abandon worldly life and take up a life of renunciation and spirituality. The first was his receiving initiation from the Holy Mother. On that auspicious day he felt an inexpressible power transmitted from her to him, which totally changed his concept of the meaning and goal of life. The second event was as follows:

One day, while showing a picture of Sri Ramakrishna Paramahamsa to Ramakrishnan, Mother said, "Both of you have the same name, yet you have become like this." These words of the Holy Mother pierced the inner depths of Ramakrishnan's heart like a lightning bolt and strengthened his desire to become a real spiritual aspirant.

One summer evening Ramakrishnan came to have darshan of the Mother during Devi Bhava. It was extremely hot inside the temple where Mother was sitting. Mother asked him to fan her. He hesitated, however, as there was a group of young ladies standing just outside the temple. He thought to himself, 'If a young man like me, an employee in the State Bank, fans a woman, they may laugh at me.' Thinking this, he didn't fan the Mother. But while coming out of the temple after Darshan, he hit his head badly on the wooden lintel over the door. Seeing his clumsiness, all the young ladies standing there burst into laughter. Ramakrishnan turned pale and felt ashamed. The next day, when Ramakrishnan went for Darshan Mother called him and said, "Yesterday you wouldn't fan me even though I asked you to. Therefore I thought it would be for your good to make you a laughing stock in front of the young ladies whose laugh you feared!" From the next Darshan on, Ramakrishnan regularly fanned Mother without being asked.

At one time, Ramakrishnan was transferred to a branch of the bank about a hundred kilometres from the ashram. One of his duties was to keep the key of the safe with him and arrive promptly at ten a.m. every morning. Leaving the ashram the following morning after the Sunday night Darshan, Ramakrishnan boarded the bus and reached a bus stop about thirteen kilometres from his office. Inquiring for another bus, he learned that there would not be any bus going to his destination before ten a.m. He then tried to get a taxi but none were available. Worried and upset, he called out "Amma!" Within a few moments, a man came along on a motorcycle and stopped in front of him. He was a complete stranger. Turning to Ramakrishnan, he said, "I am going to Pampakuda, (the very village where Ramakrishnan was working). There are no buses until after ten, so if you like, I will drop you there." Ramakrishnan gratefully climbed on the back seat, arrived at the village and walked into the bank at exactly ten o'clock! Replying to Ramakrishnan's subsequent query, Mother told him, "One call is enough if done with concentration. God will hear it."

In 1981, Ramakrishnan had an experience which taught him a good lesson of obedience to the spiritual Master. Out of fear that Ramakrishnan would become a monk if he were to live in the ashram too long, his parents tried to get him transferred to a branch bank in his home town near them. Giving in to their constant pressure, he at last submitted an application for transfer without seeking Mother's advice or permission. After some days, he changed his mind and sent a letter to the bank authorities requesting them to ignore his previous application.

One day Mother said to him, "Better inquire about the second letter you sent to the bank. It never reached the bank." Ramakrishnan replied, "That is not necessary, Mother. They must have received and accepted it." Mother insisted several times that he inquire about the second letter, but Ramakrishnan did not take her words seriously.

Before long Ramakrishnan received his transfer orders from the authorities in Trivandrum, where the head office of the bank was located. He rushed to meet the officers in charge, but it was too late. As Mother had said, they had not received any letter asking them to ignore the previous application. It had somehow been lost. In this way Ramakrishnan learned the bitter lesson that even seemingly insignificant statements of one's Guru should not be ignored.

One day in the middle of a conversation, Mother turned to Ramakrishnan with a frown on her face and said, "There are some who still look at girls, even after embracing a life of renunciation." Ramakrishnan asked, "Who is that, Mother?"

"You!" Mother replied. Ramakrishnan was shocked.

"What, me? I never look at women! Mother is scolding me for no fault of my own," he pleaded.

The next moment Mother uttered the name of a woman Ramakrishnan knew well and continued to narrate all the details of her husband's name, the names of her children and other family members. Ramakrishnan stood gaping, his mouth wide open. Hearing the exact description, whereabouts and other details of a woman the Holy Mother had no way of knowing, he stood dumbfounded. Mother again asked him, "Hey, Ramakrishnan, tell the truth! Don't you look at her every day?"

Ramakrishnan kept silent. It was true that he looked at that woman every day, but why? The woman's external appearance closely resembled the Holy Mother's. Seeing her, he felt as if he were seeing the Holy Mother herself. When Mother saw him standing there speechless with his head hanging down, she burst into laughter. It goes without saying that after this, Ramakrishnan never again looked at that woman.

The above incident clearly shows how the Holy Mother closely observes the external actions and internal thoughts of her spiritual children and instructs them accordingly.

Before the ashram was officially registered as a charitable institution, only a few people were allowed to stay there. To look after the needs of many people was impossible since there were no adequate funds at that time. Some of the brahmacharins, who had left their jobs, looked to Ramakrishnan for food and clothing. As he was still employed, he would happily meet their needs even unasked.

In the beginning days of the ashram, Ramakrishnan felt that Mother was two distinct beings, her usual self and the Divine Being during the Bhava Darshan. This idea gave rise to a lot of confusion in his mind and he would often feel miserable while thinking in this way. He at last requested Mother to bless him and clear his erroneous way of thinking. One night he had a vision of the Holy Mother in her usual mood, dressed in white clothes. This happened in the days before Mother was dressing in white. After this vision, Ramakrishnan believed that Mother was essentially the same person whatever her mood.

Ramakrishnan's faith in Mother deepened and his mind gradually became fixed on her divine form and name. This state created many troublesome situations at his work. Sometimes he made mistakes while counting out money or committed errors in the bank's accounts. In 1982, he came to live in the ashram and, at the same time, somehow continued his office work as well. Later, in 1984, he resigned his job to live in the ashram permanently.

Rao (Swami Amritatmananda Puri)

Ramesh Rao was born in a wealthy brahmana family in Haripad, Kerala. He grew up as a modern youth enjoying and indulging in worldly pleasures, following a wayward and misguided way of life. Though immersed in mundane life, he would go to a nearby Devi temple to pray and repent for his loose ways. Before undertaking any act, good or bad, he would go and pray in the temple seeking the blessings of the Divine Mother.

Once a friend of Ramesh's invited him to the Holy Mother's ashram but he declined the invitation. Later, when he was trying to go abroad for employment, he decided to visit the ashram in order to know about his future, as he had heard that the Holy Mother was endowed with divine powers and could foresee one's future. Thus, in June, 1979 he entered the temple and approached the Holy Mother during Krishna Bhava. Before he could say anything, the Holy Mother accosted him saying, "Son, you are trying to go across the ocean. Mother will make it possible if you wish. Don't worry."

At the very first meeting Ramesh was convinced of the Holy Mother's divinity and felt bound to her by a strong feeling of divine love. Returning home, he tried to concentrate his mind on the textile business which he had inherited from his father but he could not for his mind was filled only with thoughts of the Holy Mother. On some days, his yearning to see her would be so intense that he would close the shop and rush to the ashram.

One day, while taking leave of the Holy Mother to return to his house, she told him, "Son, where are you going ? You are meant to be here."

One night Ramesh had a dream of the final dissolution of the Universe; balls of fire were raining down everywhere. The ocean's waves rose up to the sky and threatened to inundate the earth. Gathering all his strength, Ramesh called out, "Amma!" Immediately a radiant light rose up from the turbulent ocean and expanded in all directions. From that effulgence emerged the enchanting form of Goddess Durga, dressed in a red silk sari and seated on a ferocious lion. She held divine weapons in each of Her eight hands. Ramesh was full of wonder to find that the compassionate face of the Goddess was the face of the Holy Mother. She consoled him saying, "Why fear when I am with you? You are My son. Don't worry." After this Ramesh had many visions of the Holy Mother in dreams.

By his close association with the Holy Mother, Ramesh's inner urge intensified to realize God and to live in the presence of the Mother. One day while sitting in her presence, he had an experience which fanned the flames of his aspiration. It was four p.m. and Ramesh had come as usual to see Mother, who was sitting in the shrine. He entered the temple and, after prostrating before the Holy Mother, he sat down near her. While he gazed at her radiant face, the whole atmosphere in the temple suddenly changed. The world of plurality vanished from his sight and only Mother was visible. He realised her to be his own Mother and found himself to be a two year old child. Intoxicated with divine love, Ramesh forgot the world. The Holy Mother lovingly placed his head on her lap. Knowing that Rao had become immersed in inner bliss, Mother gently lifted his head and had some devotees lay him on the floor of the temple. At nine p.m., Mother returned to the temple and found him still lying in that state. Only upon hearing Mother call "Son", did he return to normal consciousness.

Following this incident, Ramesh's life changed dramatically. His longing to see Mother increased. He hardly cared for worldly matters. He stopped going to the shop. His visits to the Holy Mother became frequent. He spent days and weeks at the Holy Mother's place. This sudden change in Ramesh created anxiety in his family. His parents and relations concentrated their efforts on bringing him back to worldly life and persuading him to get married. But all their attempts ended in failure. One day Mother told Ramesh, "Son, your parents are longing to see you. Go to your house and get their permission to be here." Ramesh said, "Mother, are you abandoning me? They will make trouble for me." Mother replied, "A courageous man is one who can overcome all such difficulties."

The Mother sent Rao home with another resident of the ashram. The family members used force to keep Ramesh in their custody. They thought that the Holy Mother had influenced him by using some malevolent power. In order to persuade their son to return to worldly life, they performed special rituals. The parents insisted that Ramesh eat a special type of ghee which had been prepared by a priest using particular mantras to make him leave the ashram and return to worldly life. Ramesh sought the Holy Mother's advice about the ghee. The Mother said, "Son, eat it. If there is anything evil in it, let it be. Because of your spiritual tendencies you have come to me. Nothing will happen to you, even if you eat the ghee ."

Obeying her words, Ramesh ate the ghee, but nothing happened. His thirst for spiritual life did not weaken. Now the family changed their tactics and became more harsh and inhuman. They concluded that their son's sudden change was caused by some mental abnormality arising from his disappointment at not getting a job overseas. With the assistance of his friends, who also disapproved of his new ways, they forcefully took him to a psychiatrist for treatment.

Ramesh told the doctor, "I am not crazy. I will strictly abide by the words of my Guru. It is you who are crazy for this world. Therefore, you try to impose your madness on others also." At the insistence of his relatives, the doctor treated Rao for ten days. Their aim was to shift their son toward desiring worldly life. Immediately after the psychiatric treatment, they decided to send him to Bhilai to stay with relatives, thinking that a change in environment would help him regain his old way of life. In addition, they tried to find a suitable bride for Ramesh.

In a mental predicament, Ramesh wrote to Mother, "Mother, up to this moment I have not given in to their trivial temptations. Now, if Mother doesn't save me, I will merge with the Mother in heaven. I will commit suicide."

After a month's stay at Bhilai, Rao was brought back to his house. His family was convinced by this time that he had given up his spiritual way of thinking and living. They urged him to continue his textile business. One day, without anyone's knowledge, he visited the Holy Mother pleading, "Mother, if you abandon me, I will die." Without waiting for her reply, Ramesh resumed staying in the ashram. During his short stay of three days, Mother warned him several times about his relatives' intentions to create obstacles in his path. She even advised him to go back to his house and wait till they gave their consent to take up spiritual life, but Rao paid no heed saying, "If I return home they won't let me continue my spiritual practices."

By this time, Rao's father had lodged a petition against the Holy Mother requesting police intervention to regain his son who, he asserted, was being forcibly kept in the custody of the Holy Mother. On the third day, Rao's father and some other relatives came to the ashram with a van full of policemen. Rao boldly said to the police officer, "I am mature enough to choose my way of living and am free to decide on my place of residence." They paid no attention to his words and, with the help of the police, his relatives decided to admit him to a mental hospital in Trivandrum. On their way, all of them stopped in Kollam to have their lunch. Rao refused to eat and sat in the car. Suddenly he heard a voice from within saying, "If you escape now, you will be saved. Otherwise you will be destroyed."

The very next moment an autorickshaw stopped directly in front of him. Without a moment's hesitation, he jumped into it. He told the driver the destination and asked him to drive fast. There was not even a penny in his pocket. At that time, one of the ashram residents was staying in Kollam, preparing for his Master's degree in philosophy. Rao told him what had happened. That night with the help of some devotees, Rao left Kerala, and headed for Chinmaya Mission in Bombay. Discovering that he was in Bombay, the relatives again tried to arrest him. To save his life, Rao departed for the Himalayas. He had hardly any money with him for his train fare and food, nor any warm clothes to protect him from the freezing cold. Somehow he reached the Himalayas, where he wandered from village to village. His clothes were torn and tattered as the young man became a wandering mendicant, begging his food and meditating under a tree or in a cave. Days and months passed. Finally he received a letter from the Holy Mother at an address which he had given her. She simply told him, 'Son, come back. No more problems.'

Rao returned to the Holy Mother's ashram. She then sent him to visit his parents who had learned a good lesson. They seemed to have relented and were happy to see their son back home. Yet they still tried to tempt him. When they realised that their antagonistic approach was foolish, they attempted to change him in a loving manner. But all their efforts were consumed in the fire of Rao's intense dispassion. On the twenty-seventh of August, 1982, Rao joined the ashram as a permanent resident and continued his spiritual practices undisturbed.

Nealu (Swami Paramatmananda Puri)

Neal Rosner, who was born in Chicago, USA, in the year 1949, due to his previous *samskaras*, through discrimination discovered the good and the bad effects of a worldly life right from his youth. He reached India as a detached personality. From 1968 to 1979 he stayed at Tiruvannamalai doing sadhana. He reached Vallickavu in 1979. All through the train journey he was sick and bed ridden. He suffered from diseases such as weariness, weakness, back pain, stomach pain, loss of appetite, incapability either to sit or to walk, etc.

On reaching the Ashram, after his first encounter with Amma, Nealu did not experience anything special. But the next night, during Krishna Bhava, he experienced that something very spiritual was entering into him from the old temple shrine, immersing him in bliss. Due to an unknown reason, he cried. From that he was much relieved from the pain that he had been suffering from for a long time. He entered the shrine and on looking into Mother's eyes, he saw the light of peace and inner bliss. By seeing Mother's equanimity, the torrential flow of peace emanating through Her being, by the divine experience derived from Her, he was convinced that She was a *jivanmukta* (a liberated soul). Through Her divine Grace, right at the beginning Nealu understood that Mother manifests Her divinity only during the Bhavas and that at all other times, She hides it. Nealu found himself being elevated to a plane of divine bliss. He prayed

Mother to show him the path to eternal bliss and Mother agreed to his request.

Once when Nealu asked Mother whether She could bless him with devotion for Her just by Her boon, Mother laughed innocently like a little child and said, "What can I do? I am crazy." That day when Devi Bhava was about to finish, Mother sent for Nealu, who was standing at the doorway, staring at Her. Suddenly, Nealu observed Mother's face lighting up. The brightness kept increasing until he could see nothing but radiant light all around. Everything disappeared. There was no Mother, no temple, no surrounding, no world. In the place of Mother stood a bright radiant light. That radiance or light spread covering all directions. It enveloped the entire space. Then the light kept shrinking and shrinking till it shrunk to the size of a speck of light, and finally disappeared. Nealu was baffled. He was dumbfounded. He experienced Mother's presence within him. He reached a state when the mere thought of Mother's vision of light would bring tears into his eyes. After this vision, he spent four sleepless nights. He was immersed in the divine experience. He also experienced a constant divine fragrance. He decided to do sadhana staying in Vallickavu. Amma agreed to it. Mother granted him a *rudraksha mala* (necklace). For many years, different smells emanated from the mala, at different times.

Without any medication, only through Amma's divine *sankalpa* (resolve), Nealu recovered considerably. He could now sit, stand, walk, eat, etc. He began to feel the constant presence of Mother within and also to experience a constant flow of peace and bliss.

Once he got a severe attack of cough. It was uncontrollable and unbearable. During Krishna Bhava, Mother placed Her hands over Nealu's chest and head. Then he got back the divine vision of light. He experienced that it was the same light that was within

him and that the body was not his very own (he was not identified with his body). That intoxicating divine experience lingered
within him for a very long time. With this, his disease decreased.

One evening because of severe headache, Nealu was not able
to attend the bhajans. He lied down in his room with closed eyes,
and saw before him a light which soon disappeared. He then saw
it again, and experienced Mother's divine presence. Instantly his
headache was cured, he got up and attended the bhajans.

By Amma's Grace, Nealu's physical ailments were reduced.
But much greater than this, Nealu experienced Mother's divine
presence wherever he may be, constant bliss and peace. All this
he gained through his close association with Mother. If he had
opted for *jnanamarga* (the Way of Knowledge) in Tiruvannamalai,
he now preferred *bhaktimarga* (the Way of Devotion). He states,
"This is the blessing I got from Amma." Nealu says that had there
been no severe spiritual practices for many years, he would never
have been able to understand or imbibe Mother's spiritual advice.
He firmly believes that it is only through Mother's blessings that
one can reach the goal.

In the early years, there was a severe shortage of money.
Somebody expressed their fear to Mother, "How shall we run
the Ashram?" Amma then replied, "May none of you fear. The
person who is to manage the Ashram activities will soon come
here.'" Very soon, Nealu reached the Ashram and shouldered the
financial responsibilities of the Ashram. Nealu served Mother
sincerely by paying attention even to the minutest details and
doing the service with utmost patience and *shraddha*.

Saumya (Swamini Krishnamrita Prana)

It was in 1982 that Saumya first came to stay at the Holy
Mother's Ashram. She had been interested in a spiritual life in
Australia and had lived in an ashram for several months before
journeying to India to stay at the headquarters of that Ashram
near Bombay. While living near Bombay, she had been introduced to a devotee of Amma who was at that time studying in
the Chinmaya Mission. He had talked a lot about Amma and
his experiences with Her and had said to Saumya that he felt that
she was Amma's child and that if she went to visit Her that she
would definitely want to stay there, and this was exactly what
ended up happening. After having lived in an Ashram where
there were several thousand people, many of them Westerners, it
was a profound and delightful shock for Saumya to visit Amma's
humble little Ashram where there were only 14 living there at the
time, in a few thatched huts.

Having been informed by the devotee in a letter that Saumya
would be visiting, Amma rushed over to hug her when she first
entered the darshan hut. Saumya was astounded by the love and
tenderness that Amma was showing to her. In the Ashrams that
she had been in one could only prostrate and touch the Guru's
sandals while the Guru sat untouched at a safe distance, but
here was Amma tenderly caressing her devotees with a love and
compassion that Saumya had never known existed

In those days Amma sometimes acted like a crazy girl and
would lie down in the sand, or eat food off of the ground. She
would often go into samadhi while singing bhajans or simply
giving darshan to the people. Amma lived so simply giving all
Her time to God and the people, every hour of the day. There
was nothing for Herself. She would sit in the sand lost in loving
God, crying to God, singing to God all the time. God was Her

only focus, and when She wasn't immersed in God, She was loving us, loving everyone. She couldn't hide this love because it was oozing out of every pore of Her body.

Before coming to Amma Saumya had thought that she would one day have a family and she had loved to travel, but these desires totally fell away after meeting Amma. After hearing the spiritual truths from Amma that this birth was meant only to realize God, she felt she could not go back and live in the West and pretend that that life was real. She wanted to live with Amma as her Guru and for Amma to discipline her.

After a short time of living in the Ashram, Amma asked Saumya to take over the position of attending to Her needs during the Bhava darshans. This was a great honor and a pleasure most times but also very difficult as she didn't understand Malayalam. One of her duties was to wipe Amma's face during the Devi Bhava. Although Her Body never perspired Her face would sometimes be moist from the sweat of Her devotees, as the temple was always very hot and crowded, and Amma liked to have Her face wiped after every one or two people for the convenience of those coming for darshan.

Saumya often dreaded wiping the face of the Divine Mother of the Universe with a face towel, but she had no choice as at that time Amma never did this for Herself.

Devi Amma used to appear to Saumya at night in her dreams glaring at her as she was lying down sleeping, and asking her if she wasn't going to wipe Her face for Her. These dreams were so real that Saumya would jump up in bed and sometimes start searching for Her face towels, feeling very guilty because she had been lying down sleeping. Sometimes another girl would be sharing the room with her overnight and would inquire what she was doing in the dark in the middle of the night.

When she finally woke up and realized that it was the middle of the night and that Devi Bhava had finished and it was really all a dream, she would apologize to Amma for lying down and going back to sleep as what else could she do? These dreams used to happen at least once a week and sometimes even three times a week and went on for several years before finally stopping.

When she first came to Amma she wanted to learn how to lead a spiritual life after having seen the impermanence of any kind of joy found in a worldly life. In the early years of the Ashram, Amma used to talk about service, but Saumya never thought that this was including her in any way. Then as the years went by Amma seemed to talk about service more and more. Gradually the desire to perform service to the world grew and blossomed from the small seed that Amma planted in Saumya's heart and lovingly nurtured with Her love and attention. Now it has become the strongest desire in her heart. Her secret prayer is "Amma give me the strength and purity to be able to serve the world."

Madhu (Swami Premananda Puri)

Madhu was born in Réunion (a French colony), and was of Indian origin. Right from childhood he had an intense desire to take *sannyas*.

In 1976, Madhu reached India and got acquainted with the Ramakrishna ashram. He asked Swami Vireshwarananda of the Belur Math whether he could get to the Himalayas to do sadhana. Swamiji asked him to go to southern India as it was best suited to Madhu. As per his instructions, he was doing spiritual practices in Arunachala when one devotee told him, "You seem to be a Kali devotee. Kali is in Vallickavu. Go visit her."

That was how Madhu happened to reach Vallickavu on 1ˢᵗ June 1980. It was during Bhava time. Inside the old temple shrine, Mother told Gayatri, "My son Madhu is waiting outside. Go and bring him in." On stepping inside the temple and seeing Mother, Madhu burst into tears. Mother told Madhu, "Since how long have I been waiting for you."

Next day, Mother, holding a photo of Vireshwarananda, began asking everybody whose photo it was. Madhu who sat next to Mother said, "It is Vireshwaranandaji." Amma replied, "He is a nice man." Amma told Madhu that she saw him during meditation. Wasn't he foresighted in sending Madhu to South India! During Devi Bhava, Mother gave mantra diksha to Madhu.

In 1982, Madhu celebrated Amma's birthday in Reunion. By establishing a branch of Mata Amritanandamayi Math in Reunion, Madhu engaged himself in propagating the Sanatana Dharma (eternal religion). Madhu was a good sadhak who possessed qualities like humility, scholarship (knowledge), compassion, and good capacity to work.

Madhusudan who got brahmacharya deeksha on 24ᵗʰ February 1985 under Amma's instructions, became Prematma Chaitanya. Madhu proved his loyalty towards Mother saying thus, "It is Amma who made me what I am. Had I not met Mother, I might have led an ordinary worldly life. It is only due to Mother's grace that I could stick to the path of renunciation. Much more than individual capacity, it is the Guru's Grace that is important for spiritual progress."

Chapter Thirteen

Mother as the Spiritual Master

W ho is a perfect person? If this question is asked to a modern youth he would say that an ideal person is a handsome, highly influential multimillionaire or perhaps a high ranking political leader; otherwise he would say the names of some romantic looking movie stars or cricket players. It is a pity that today the youngsters cannot conceive of a society without movies, politics and romance. It is a vital force for them. But do these have anything to do with our life and character building? What makes a person beautiful and perfect? What adds sweetness and attractiveness to one's actions? What is that factor which makes one immortal and adorable? Is it any of the afore-said things? A mature person endowed with discrimination will undoubtedly say, "No, absolutely not!" Then what is it? To put it in a sentence, it is the integration of inner virtues which in turn will manifest as eternal virtues through one's whole being. This is what one can experience in the presence of the Holy Mother Amritanandamayi, the beautiful blending of unconditional love and bliss.

People from different walks of life, each according to their own level of understanding and mental maturity speak differently about the Holy Mother. For example, if you ask who Mata Amritanandamayi is to a person whose intellect always dwells at a gross level, he would say, "She is an extraordinary woman who can cure terrible and incurable diseases by a mere touch or look." He may also say, "She can also solve your worldly problems and can easily fulfil all your desires." If the same question is asked to one who has a more subtle intellect he would say, "O, the Holy Mother is really incredible. She can bestow on you many psychic powers. She is a master in telepathy and clairvoyance. It is nothing for her to transform water into panchamritam and milk. All the eight mystic powers are under her sway," and so on. A true spiritual seeker's answer to the same question would be, "The Mother is the Ultimate Goal to be realised by an aspirant. She is the source and support of true seekers and helps them to cross the ever-changing Ocean of Transmigration. Her very nature is love and compassion; she is a veritable witness to the truths expressed in the Vedas and all other religious texts of the world. If you take refuge at her feet, definitely the Goal is at hand. She is a Perfect Master and a Great Mother as well."

From the standpoint of a person who is following the Path of Devotion (Bhakti Yoga), the Holy Mother is a true devotee par excellence. In her one can see the different aspects of Supreme Devotion manifesting unimpeded. When one who pursues the Path of Knowledge (Gnana Yoga) observes the Mother, he can perceive a perfect Knower of the Self in her words and deeds. For a person who is sincerely following the Path of Action (Karma Yoga), the Holy Mother is unsurpassed among Karma Yogins. These are all partial views born of each one's limited experience and understanding. But through close association and observation devoid of prejudice and presumption, one could clearly comprehend that the Holy Mother is an integration of all these.

There is a proverb in Malayalam, 'As patient as the Earth.' The Mother Earth bears everything. People kick her, spit on her, till her with a plough, dig into her, and cut open her breast using a pick axe for cultivation and other purposes. They even construct hundred story buildings on her but she patiently bears everything. She has no complaints. She despises none but serves and nourishes all in the best way. Likewise, the Holy Mother shows an immense amount of patience in rebuilding the character of her children. She patiently waits until the disciples become mature enough to be disciplined. Until then, she bathes them in her selfless love forgiving all the errors which they may commit.

If one closely goes through the great lineage of the ancient saints and sages of India and observes the ways which they adopted to teach and enlighten their disciples, it is not difficult to understand the unique nature of the Guru-disciple relationship which cannot be seen anywhere else in the world. The Holy Mother would say, "In the beginning a Satguru (Perfect Master) won't give strict instructions to his disciple. He will simply love him. He will bind the disciple with his unconditional love. The strong impact created by the Guru's love will make the disciple fit for the Guru to work on his vasanas or mental tendencies. Slowly the Guru, with strict yet loving instructions, will discipline and remould the disciple's personality. In a real Guru-disciple relationship, it will be difficult to distinguish who is the Guru and who is the disciple because the Guru will be humbler than the disciple and the disciple will be humbler than the Guru." In the beginning the Guru, in addition to showing great love for the disciple, may even act according to the disciple's whims and fancies to some extent, but when he finds that the disciple is mature enough to earnestly start spiritual practice then the Guru will slowly start disciplining him. Once the disciplining starts however, though full of love for his disciple who is verily like a son or daughter to him or her, he will not express his love much. His sole aim will be to make the disciple aware of his own Pure Self. In other words, his disciplining itself is another way of expressing his love. That is real love, transforming the disciple into a pure jewel.

Pointing out and correcting the drawbacks of her children the Holy Mother would say, "I am like a gardener. The garden is full of colourful flowers. I was not asked to look after the beautiful flowers which are in no way defective but I have been asked to remove the insects and worms from the pest-ridden flowers and plants. To remove the insects I may have to pinch the petals and leaves which is painful, but it is only to save the plants and flowers from destruction. In the same way, Mother will always work with the children's weaknesses. The process of elimination is painful but it is for your good. The virtuous aspects need no attention, but if your weaknesses are not removed, they will destroy your virtues as well. My children, you may think that Mother is angry with you. Not at all. Mother loves you more than anyone else and that is why she does all these things. Mother expects nothing except your spiritual progress."

One could never see the Holy Mother sitting on a royal seat commanding her spiritual children and devotees to do this and that. She instructs and at the same time sets an example by her actions. Humility and simplicity are the trademarks of greatness. The Holy Mother is a living example of this. She is humbler than the humblest and simpler than the simplest. She says about herself, "I am the servant of servants. This life is for others. Her children's happiness is Mother's wealth and health."

The Holy Mother's method of exhausting the ego and other negative tendencies of her children is wonderful. She is always the invincible warrior. The Mother herself prepares the field to test her children's mental maturity and spiritual progress by creating a suitable situation. Without causing the least suspicion she leads one to the field. By the time one realizes the seriousness of the situation, all the inner foes rise up and the discriminating intellect gives way to the emotional mind. At this moment the Holy Mother properly uses the opportunity to remove the egoism of her children. Her mighty weapons hit the target without fail and in due course the negative tendencies of those who seek her guidance become weaker and weaker. The following is one such incident.

Once, some years ago Brahmachari Nealu brought a portable typewriter from Tiruvannamalai where he had previously resided. Although Balu had not learned typing, he took a piece of paper and just for the fun of it typed, 'Mother, make me your slave.' Mother, who was sitting nearby talking to Nealu suddenly turned towards Balu and asked, "Son, what are you typing?" Balu thereupon translated the meaning of the sentence into Malayalam for her. Without asking or saying anything more about it, the Mother continued to talk to Nealu.

After fifteen minutes Mother said to Nealu, "I am going to send Balu abroad." It was a shock for Balu to hear those words from Mother's mouth as he had already quit two jobs with the intention of staying in Mother's presence forever. "What did you say, Mother?" he anxiously asked.

"Yes, we need money to run the ashram. The number of residents is increasing and we have no income to support them all. So, you must go and work," Mother replied.

This was enough for Balu. His inner foes raised their hoods and with vehemence he said, "No, I don't want to work. I cannot go away from here. I came here to stay with Mother and not to do worldly work or earn money." However, Mother went on insisting that he must go until his anger knew no bounds. His negative tendencies stood ready to attack.

Suddenly in a soft voice Mother said, "Son, what did you type just a few minutes ago? If you want to become God's servant, you have to surrender all that is yours at His Feet. If the mind is not pure, God won't dwell in your heart. To become God's servant is to accept all experiences, good and bad, auspicious and inauspicious, with an equipoised mind. See everything as God's Will. Son, I don't want your wealth. When I see you crying for God I am so happy and my heart overflows towards you." As soon as she uttered the last word she became absorbed into a divine mood. Tear drops rolled down her cheeks and her body became still. This continued for an hour after which she slowly came down to this plane of worldly existence.

Balu's mind was full of remorse. He fell at her feet and begged her to forgive him. He prayed, "Mother, please purify my heart. Rid me of all impure thoughts and actions. Make me a perfect instrument in your hands." She consoled him and said, "Son, don't worry. You have come to Mother and now it is her responsibility to look after you and make you perfect." Hearing these words, Balu felt full of peace and joy.

The Holy Mother once said, "Children, you are happy if Mother always shows a smiling face. If Mother says something against your wish, then you will think that Mother has no love towards you, but it is not so. Mother is always trying to make you stronger. To reinforce you spiritually all mental weaknesses should be removed. To achieve that end sometimes she will make an external show of anger. Sometimes this is necessary in order to teach you. Take for example a cow that is merrily eating up the tender leaves of a young coconut tree. It is not enough if one says, 'Dear cow, please don't eat the tender leaves. The plant will wither away.' The cow definitely won't move an inch. But if you take a long stick and shout at it, 'Go away, go away!' the cow will immediately end its mischief. The same is true with Mother's show of anger. Children, Mother has not even an iota of anger towards you. Always remember that Mother has no selfish motives and acts only for your spiritual progress. If Mother always shows her love and affection to you then you won't look inwards to seek your Real Self. Children, as far as a worldly person is concerned, it is enough for him to look after his wife and children, but a real sannyasin on the other hand, has to shoulder the burden of the whole world. Therefore you must grow stronger."

On one occasion after the usual darshan, Mother could go for rest only at about four a.m. After she had entered her hut and laid down after closing the door, one ashramite slept in front of her room as usual in order to ensure that nobody would disturb her by going into the room. Exactly at that time a young woman who had missed the bus and had walked all the way from Kollam, a distance of thirty-five kilometres, reached the ashram seeking Mother's blessings. When she learned that Mother had gone to bed she was crestfallen but still with a glimmer of hope she called Mother aloud a couple of times. Hearing the lady's voice, the ashramite who was lying down in front of Mother's door got up and scolded the lady for disturbing Mother and even asked her to leave the place. At that very moment, Mother, who could understand what was happening, opened the door and came out to meet the devotee. After affectionate inquiries, the Mother consoled her and assured her of solving the problems which she was facing.

Turning to the person who had slept in front of her door, Mother spoke in a serious tone, "I am not here for enjoying any rest or comfort but rather to serve others and alleviate their sufferings. Their happiness is my happiness. I do not want anyone's service. I am here to serve all. I must be free to meet anybody at any time. I won't permit anyone to prevent me from meeting the devotees who come seeking solace and succor from me. Do you know with what great difficulty they come here with their meagre savings just to unburden their aching heart to me? If you repeat this rudeness and try to impose rules on me that I should meet devotees only at such and such times I will dissolve this organization. I do not want any such thing as a mission if it is not to serve ailing humanity. A mission should be for service." Saying this, she prohibited the ashramite and all of the other residents from sleeping in front of her hut.

On another occasion a sick lady who had come to the ashram for Mother's advice had vomited on Mother's cloth. A resident, one of the girls who was personally attending on Mother, picked up the dirtied cloth with a stick and was about to hand it over to the washerman. Seeing this, Mother scolded the girl and said, "If you are unable to see the one Divine in all and serve all equally, then what is the use of having done so many years of meditation and service? Is there any difference between me and this sick lady?" Saying these words, Mother took the cloth herself and washed it, prohibiting the girl from attending on her for some days afterwards.

The Holy Mother's mere presence itself is inspiring to the devotees. She can inspire and give them the strength to do anything and everything at any time. For example, if there is some work in the ashram such as carrying bricks, sand and other materials for construction purposes or even emptying the septic tank, cleaning the ashram premises or assisting the masons in concrete work, etc., the residents would run here and there trying to gather some devotees to help. Sometimes it might be three or four in the morning when the Bhava Darshan had finished and all the devotees would be ready to go to sleep. Suddenly the Holy Mother would come to where the work was going to proceed. She would always be the first to start the work. Despite the fact that she had been sitting from six o'clock the previous evening until three or four the next morning she would be seen working full of cheer and enthusiasm. Very soon word would spread that Mother is carrying bricks, water or whatever it may be and from all directions the devotees would come running. The most interesting part of it is that the work which normally would have taken six or seven hours to finish would be completed within one or two hours.

In order to make the devotees forget the strain of the work, the Holy Mother will make the devotees laugh with her great sense of humour and will even make a small fire near the work spot and make drinks and roast peanuts for all those who are working and herself distribute them to her devotees. In the midst of the work the Holy Mother will instruct everyone saying, "Children, while engaged in any kind of work always try to chant your mantra or sing devotional songs. Only those actions which are surrendered to the Lord are counted as real action and then action (karma) becomes Yoga. Otherwise it is Karma Bhoga (action motivated by the urge to enjoy)."

"Even when the Gopis of Vrindavan went out to sell milk, buttermilk, etc., they would call out 'Krishna, Madhava, Yadava, Kesava...' Even in the kitchen they would write and affix Krishna's different names on all the spice bottles and other provisions. They also discharged the duties of a housewife. They never sat idle but always carried Krishna's form in their heart and His Divine Names on their lips. Children, try to be like them."

Whatever questions are asked and whoever is the questioner, whether a theist, an atheist, a rationalist or an antagonist, the Holy Mother gently, calmly, and affectionately answers them without hurting them or belittling their ideas. For example, one day a young man who visited the Ashram told the Holy Mother, "I have no faith at all in spiritual philosophy and spiritual masters. Is it not better to serve humanity? Many people are suffering from

poverty and starvation. What are these so-called spiritualists doing for them? Are they not simply wasting their time sitting idle?"

The Holy Mother calmly replied, "Son, what you say is correct. Of course, service to humanity is important. A true spiritual
seeker's life must be dedicated to that. Mother perfectly agrees
with that point of yours. But what is real service? Real service is
extending help without expecting anything. Who is doing that?
If somebody has an idea to help a poor family undoubtedly there
will be a selfish motive behind it. Everyone is after name and fame.
Mother knows that spiritual advice won't satisfy the hunger of a
person who is plunged in poverty. We must have compassion and
love for such people. Real compassion and love will come only
by practising spirituality. We must have a high ideal in our life.
We must be ready to sacrifice everything to uphold that ideal.
This is genuine spirituality. Simply providing food will not solve
anyone's problems either. Again one will be in want of food. So
the best way is to help others both externally and internally, i.e.
feed them and at the same time make them aware of the necessity
to develop internally as well. This is possible only through spiritual education. This kind of service will help one to lead a happy
and balanced life in any circumstance even if one is starving. In
reality spirituality is that which teaches us how to lead a perfect
life in the world. Son, everything depends on the mind. If the
mind is calm and tranquil even the lowest hell will become an
abode of happiness but if the mind is agitated even the highest
of heavens will become a place of tremendous suffering. That is
what one gets from spirituality and spiritual masters, peace and
tranquillity without which one cannot live."

Even the most notorious fellow, who in the eyes of his own
parents and close relatives is cruel and who has been hated by
them, is a darling son to the Holy Mother. Even such a person
would say, "Mother loves me the most. I love her more than

my own mother who gave birth to me. I am her child." This is the impression created by the Holy Mother in the hearts of her devotees. Even about a rogue the Holy Mother would say, "What a good son he is. He is very innocent." Overlooking their bad qualities, she will speak highly of their goodness which in reality may be only infinitesimal.

Through our direct experience we can realize that the Holy Mother is a fountain of inexhaustible spiritual energy and dynamic creativity. Though the Holy Mother keenly attends to both the spiritual and material needs of her devotees, she still remains detached and as pure as ever.

To express devotion and gratefulness, a devotee may remark, "O Mother, you are so compassionate to me. Because of your grace I am having good meditation and my mind is perfectly peaceful." Someone else will say, "O Mother, because of your blessings, all my family problems are now solved and many of my lifelong wishes have been fulfilled." Hearing these words of the devotees, the Holy Mother sometimes will laugh loudly and reply, "Namah Shivaya! Who is Mother to bless anyone? She is just a crazy girl who is wandering around because there is nobody to put her in a lunatic asylum. I am not doing anything. God does everything without doing anything."

There are many differences among the people who come to visit the Holy Mother. Some will ask questions about Kundalini Yoga (techniques to awaken the serpent power), while others are curious to know about Nirvikalpa Samadhi, the state of abiding in the Supreme Self. The next person may complain about bad health. Some parents will come crying saying that their only son is totally misled and doing all kinds of wicked actions and will ask the Mother to save him. Some young people will complain that although they had finished their studies long ago, they couldn't find a job. They will say, "Please Mother, bless me to get a job."

Husbands will come saying that their wife is not sincere. Wives will say that their husband is not loving them. There are some people who pray to Mother to punish their neighbor or who will tell her that their cow is not giving enough milk or the coconut trees in their yard are not bearing an abundance of coconuts. Some seek her blessings to pass their examinations while others will come with an incurable disease. Some parents are distraught because their son is showing a tendency to take up to a life of renunciation. There are a few who will become serious spiritual practitioners after meeting the Holy Mother and come to seek her direct guidance in order to proceed with their sadhana. In this way one can see the whole world coming to seek her bless-ings. The Holy Mother discards none. Each one of them will be treated equally giving the same amount of love and affection and will be instructed in accordance with their mental maturity and need. She not only listens to their problems but bestows fulfill-ment of all desires.

Every morning around nine o'clock, the Holy Mother comes to meet the devotees who come in large numbers to have her darshan. Calling each one near her, she will keenly listen to their problems. The Holy Mother would say, "Children, I need nothing from you except your burden of sorrows. Mother is here to shoulder it." She will sit there until everyone is received and consoled. Almost everyday she finishes the darshan only by two or three o'clock in the afternoon. Returning to the room, the Mother will go through all the mail or give instructions to the residents. She will be engaged in giving necessary advice about the management of the ashram administration. Even while eat-ing she will be instructing someone or reading somebody's letter. Oftentimes she will call a family or a person who came too late for darshan. If it is a Bhava Darshan day then she will again come at around five o'clock in the evening to lead devotional singing.

After the singing, the Bhava Darshan will begin which might last until three or four the next morning. Until then, the Holy Mother will be seated in the temple receiving the devotees one by one and listening to their problems, whether spiritual or worldly. She not only listens to them but also solves their problems by mere touch, look, or through a pure sankalpa (resolve). The Holy Mother Amritanandamayi is a unique phenomenon even in this sacred land of India. Assuming the Bhava of Adi Parashakti (Divine Mother), the Primal Supreme Energy, she ceaselessly serves the Lord's Creation with her every breath. In the spiritual history of India, she stands unparalleled in her limitless manifestation of Grace and Compassion for erring humanity. May her divine life serve as a guiding star for all those who aspire to realize Supreme Peace and the Bliss of Self-Realisation.

Om Namah Shivaya

CPSIA information can be obtained
at www.ICGtesting.com
Printed in the USA
FSHW020009220519
58342FS

9 781680 377545